MOVE THE SALE FORWARD

Position Yourself
And Your Business
To Make Things Happen

John Klymshyn

SILVER LAKE PUBLISHING
LOS ANGELES, CALIFORNIA

Move the Sale Forward
Position Yourself and Your Business to Make Things Happen
First edition
Copyright © 2003 by Silver Lake Publishing

Silver Lake Publishing
2025 Hyperion Avenue
Los Angeles, California 90027

For a list of other publications or for more information, please call
1.888.663.3091. In Alaska and Hawaii and outside of the United
States, please call 1.323.663.3082.

Library of Congress Catalogue Number: pending

Move the Sale Forward
Position Yourself and Your Business to Make Things Happen.
Includes index.
Pages: 282

ISBN: 1-56343-769-4
Printed in the United States of America.

Acknowledgments

No book is a lone endeavor. Many people have impacted my life, many have helped me to maintain committed to my ideas; others have been directly involved in the shaping, selection or removal of the words considered for this book.

Here is a very short list of the folks who really chipped in, and to whom I owe great thanks:

Ken Keller for making the connection.

Jim Walsh for making the commitment.

Kristin Loberg for making the deadline.

Ed Friedman for assistance in clarifying and articulating the vision.

Tim Pulte for proving it all to be true.

Bill Hobson, Chuck Kokoska and Tony Winterowd for prayers and accountability.

Phil Meany, Greg Sherwood, John Lesinski and all of the G&E team for their enthusiasm.

Paul Linder for uncompromising faith.

Matt Banes for frequent word-smithing.

Mark Gillett and Mary Rasenberger for dotting the *i*'s.

Karen Fitzgerald for destroying the boundaries.

My wife Terri, for quieting the beast.

My daughter Lauren, for not letting me complain (and for lending the laptop).

And my son John III for his superhuman strength.

I dedicate this book to everyone searching for connection in business, and in life.

The journey I have traveled from the first time I was asked: "Have you ever thought about writing a book?" to when we typed the final pages has been fun, challenging and one filled with the ever-advancing development of ideas, beliefs and convictions. This book is proof positive that passion for an idea is an unstoppable force.

John Klymshyn
Santa Clarita, California
January, 2003

ABOUT THE AUTHOR

John Klymshyn has been involved in business-to-business selling for more than 18 years. He has published more than 75 articles for various trade publications and newspapers, and spends most of his time traveling internationally, presenting an average of 80 seminars per year to thousands of sales and non-sales professionals.

People ask: *What makes a salesperson successful?*

Is selling a science?

Is the ability to sell inherent or can it be learned?

Klymshyn addresses all of these questions with clear, concise and thought-provoking answers, challenging us to view selling as a natural by-product of understanding human nature.

Klymshyn, through his training seminars and coaching sessions, has impacted the professional skill level of tens of thousands of sales professionals.

He now brings to this book a proven, immediate way to dismantle the barriers to successful selling by giving you the tools and ammunition to move relationships forward. Klymshyn has hit on something so basic that it's shocking that experts and academics alike have overlooked it for years. It's simply: *Move the conversation forward by practiced and logical increments, and success will follow.* Klymshyn doesn't teach *selling*; he helps you to manage relationships so people buy from you with confidence.

Move the Sale Forward

As a former radio talk show host, sales manager and consummate sales professional, Mr. Klymshyn's training methods for more successful selling have been embraced by sales and marketing professionals across a wide spectrum of industries, ranging from advertising, to commercial real estate, to employment and staffing services, to consulting services, to travel and hospitality sales.

Klymshyn has offered his seminars at various universities and presented his techniques on training tomorrow's sales force at the University of Southern California. He has also conducted classes for the University of California Los Angeles Extension Center for Business and Management, where he received one of the highest instructor ratings of the semester.

Born and raised in New York, Klymshyn currently lives with his wife and two children in Santa Clarita, California. His goal is to continue to teach management and sales teams the powerful, human approach to increasing sales presented in this book.

TABLE OF CONTENTS

FOREWORD

Many authors have tried to convince the public of the professionalism of the salesperson and the selling process. None has demonstrated an ability to do it as well as John Klymshyn in this treatise. He not only justifies the mantle of selling as an honorable profession, but he brings into it the impact of emotion, similar to that which exists in our "honorable" professions of medicine and law.

In a most difficult and changing economy, entry-level opportunities point to sales in so many ways. This book gives one the understanding as to what those opportunities are, and how they may be maximized as one enters the field. Several students of marketing are enamored by the marketing concept, but fail to understand that it all begins with the customer. The quickest way to understand the customer is to deal with him or her across the table—seller to buyer. Concepts such as being a good listener and asking open-ended killer questions, as Klymshyn relates in this book, are then honed with each meeting.

While medicine and law are held up as the honorable professions, there is a definite element of sales in each. Bedside manner is another way of talking about the art of listening and sales. Closing arguments before a jury are the same as the art of the close that he analyzes. Convincing one to see a situation your way is selling at its most basic.

From a basic understanding of the sales process, and with practice, one can move in so many directions. Sales is the key responsibility of everyone in a company from the chief executive officer to the warehouseman. Contact with the customer is at many points and each level one needs to understand how to *move the process forward*, as he so aptly puts it.

Additionally, Klymshyn relates the anatomy of conversation, and delves into the details that can make or break the deal. He has had such great experience that his examples are real, and very well thought through, as well as being easy to grasp. Good sales people have an innate ability to break something down to its most simplistic form, and the author has done just that throughout.

Klymshyn is able to personalize the sales process in a manner similar to the way he works himself. He is a master at moving the process forward, and has now shown the ability to put that process on paper so even the youngest neophytes in the sales business can follow it. In addition, he has *put* the right kind of emotion into the concept of selling, rather than *taking it out*, as most would want to do.

This is a book not written by an academic for academics, but rather written for practicing and soon-to-be practicing sales people by a practicing sales professional. John Klymshyn knows his material; he is able to break it down to its basic components and is able to relate it in such a manner that all can comprehend. There is emotion, personalization and reality in what he says and how he says it. This book is one for the ages.

Professor James G. Ellis
University of Southern California
The Marshall School of Business

Introduction: Moving Forward

When you think of moving forward, you probably think of things you do every day: walking, working, building relationships, rearing children, setting goals, checking off lists…and growing older. It's something you do intuitively in order to reach a goal, accomplish something and feel a sense of completion. Is forward motion spiritual? In a sense. Is it physical? To an extent. Is it available to all? Absolutely. But it can be hard to apply to everything in life, including the sales profession.

Whether you're a frontline newcomer or the CEO of a major corporation, forward motion is what drives you out of bed in the morning, inspires you to finish a project, urges you to make a phone call to someone you've never met and encourages you to work for that opportunity to demonstrate your talents. This book will add to your repertoire of talents and arm you with a sharper set of selling tools…and a renewed competitive spirit.

You also move conversations forward as you solve problems, answer questions and create better and new ideas. What does *moving the sale forward* mean? It means taking this simple concept of moving forward and applying it to the sales profession. Moving the sale forward has to do with closing—securing a sale by guiding it from beginning to end with flow and consistency. This is not an easy task. Moving forward in sales can be equally as challenging as moving forward in life; it takes patience, practice and a few good tools. This book aims to teach you how to move sales forward and get to where you want to be as a sales professional with enthusiasm, focus and tenacity.

Sales and Salesmen

From a sales approach, forward motion generates millions of dollars for sales people, sales managers, entrepreneurs and others across the U.S. each year. Some of these people will share their success stories in these pages. Many of the sales concepts outlined in this book don't necessarily apply to sales alone. Having good listening skills, patience and the ability to communicate effectively with other people, for example, are skills we all need to succeed in life—whether we're doctors or sellers of hospital equipment.

Understanding what someone else needs and trying to meet those needs are basic human endeavors. Knowing how to sell yourself is also a skill everyone needs to learn. There are underlying concepts to these skills and you can master them.

For those who are in sales and use these skills on a daily basis, it's important to review the tools required in order to maintain the passion for the sales profession. As we'll see by looking at the experiences of others, understanding and applying these ideas and concepts ultimately leads to a reduction in stress, an increased contact with people and greater income.

Every salesperson experiments with different selling methods, and most find the business of selling to be a magical, thrilling, high-wire act that attracts a small percentage of the overall population. It is not for everyone, but for the few who are sales professionals, this is the book to keep on your desk.

The sales profession has had a history of stereotypes working against it. Some of those include the notion that sales people are unscrupulous men and women who exploit and manipulate others only to get what they want. This is not true, as this book will show.

The people you'll meet and the ideas you'll be exposed to do not follow any stereotype. Sales professionals are as equally passionate, honest and giving as anyone else in any other profession. If you're already a salesperson, you know this, and you make a difference in the world that is visible to your families, employers and clients.

Selling

So what is *selling*? How does it apply to someone who doesn't work to earn commissions? How do you know if you are right for the profession? How can you keep your enthusiasm through a potentially long sales cycle? These are good questions, the answers to which we will address, in addition to these others:

- How can you learn to persuade, without coming off as though you are trying to exploit and manipulate?

- How can you involve and engage others?

- What do you need to do to get people to hear you out?

- How do you create and, more importantly, maintain forward motion?

- How will the concept of forward motion help you be more effective—more engaging—as a sales professional as well as a parent, spouse, manager, leader and person in general?

- What is the difference between the approach this book presents and any other approach to connecting with people, running a business, closing more sales and ultimately succeeding in life?

The problem with traditional sales training is that the priorities are misaligned. Sellers want to sell goods or services at a price that benefits them and allows them to move product; buyers want to receive a useful product or service at a reasonable price and feel good about it. It's not about making the seller happy, although some buyers fall into this trap.

The question: How do you get people to buy from you, without making them feel pressured? Simply put, a sales professional must make the transaction of buying and selling as mutually beneficial as possible. To do this requires a certain set of practical tools and the capacity to make human connections on a new level. This book will help you gather these tools and learn how to make those human connections.

Move the Sale Forward

One thing you'll learn, which is contrary to traditional sales training, is that as a seller, your goal should not be the closing of the sale. Your goal should not be to make more money, either. These goals will leave you short of reaching the ultimate goal: finding those people with whom you can truly connect, and as a result conduct effective business. This, in turn, allows you to enjoy your work more, manage your team more effectively, make more money and experience less stress in your life.

Sales is an honorable and important profession. It's a driving force in any economy. To understand the power of selling is to understand the power of commerce and society's reliance on simple exchanges. Money for product, service for money or even service for product. Selling widgets, digits, content and services drives markets up and down, out of the past and into the future. It is the essential lifeblood of any capitalist society. And it doesn't require a fancy Ivy League degree or MBA.

Everyone has something to sell in some manner or form. Everyone has information to move forward and affect someone else. But the act of selling takes an amazing skill. Moving the spark of an idea to fruition and winning others' help in the process is a great skill to have. The essence of receiving compensation for the delivery of good or services is a *sale*. When you get hired, for example, you have sold yourself.

Sales is not something you will find as a degree program at universities across America. One sales degree program of which I am aware is part of the Fisher School of Business at the University of Ohio. But the Fisher School program is an exception to the rule that academia—and even the business establishment—doesn't treat sales like a profession. Lawyers are considered professionals. So are accountants, physicians, even bankers. But not sales people.

Having said that, it's important to note that true sales professionals never find themselves out of work. They don't have caps on their incomes. They move freely among vertical markets, various networking opportunities and industries. How many professionals can switch their specialty in mid-career and thrive? A doctor in dermatology won't suddenly switch to ophthalmology; but a sales professional can easily switch from selling pharmaceuticals to selling Internet-based technology.

This freedom of movement is what makes sales so exciting and re-warding. Moreover, the skills you acquire as a salesperson transfer to other activities in your life as a parent, civic leader and friend. You are about to learn about the process of selling. In this book, you will find that moving sales—and conversations—forward is key to the livelihood of every business, organization, group or family.

Economics

Whatever the economy is doing or not doing on the day you open this book, the philosophy presented between these covers will carry you through to an increased sense of control and peace of mind when it comes to selling. No matter the economic climate, sales will continue to be the driving force of the economy, which makes sales professionals all the more vital every day of the year.

Sales professionals can influence markets and shift the course of what consumers want. They do this by affecting the microcosm of markets—by having an impact on how consumers think and what they buy and how they make decisions about their money.

Ask yourself:

- What people do I see come in and out of my place of business on a regular basis who can benefit from more of my services?

- What can I bring into my company that will have a useful impact on it?

- What do I see happening in the community that a few more hands would not positively impact?

This book is the antidote to traditional sales thinking. It is the antithesis of the smarmy sales approach. After 15 years in the sales world, I have arrived at the best methods for selling and selling well. I have learned through the process of trial and (multiple) error. Having made over 250,000 cold calls myself, I know what it takes to maintain focus, enthusiasm and charisma through a long sales cycle and some tough times.

I know how to keep the selling spirit and competitive edge, because no matter the economic climate, you can always sell, persuade, manage and lead. I share this knowledge here in the hopes that readers take away a new set of tools for selling into the future.

Traditional Language and Concepts

Two things you must be willing to accept at the start of this book:

1) You must be open to learning something new by way of a new language; and

2) You must be open to learning something new by rejecting old concepts.

Like other professions, sales uses its own language and jargon. Starting in Chapter 1, the basics of the language will be presented. For the seasoned salesperson, some words will sound familiar but may carry new meaning; others will be new additions to your vocabulary. We cannot make a *human connection*, for example, unless we understand what *closing* really means. Certain phrases, words and expressions will become familiar to you throughout this book.

Once we explore the language, we will discuss the use of that language to achieve a new set of goals—a new standard of objectives and concepts. During my early years as a sales person, I found the traditional approaches to selling hard to practice, and having them shoved down my throat did not make the task any easier.

Not only did I find it hard to get people to buy from me, but I didn't find any of the selling techniques useful or comfortable to work with. Take, for example, the following idea (i.e., imagine having a boss tell you how to sell by saying this): "Make them understand! When the potential customer tells you: "I don't have the money right now," they mean "I don't want to take the time to think about it right now." Approaching potential customers with this manipulative scheme left me squirming. It's not fun to sell anything based on the notion that selling is about what you can get out of a customer rather than what the customer really wants and needs.

Let's look at a quick example, assuming you're the potential buyer. If I call you to try to sell you something, you might resist because it's my idea, and not yours. If I have a ready response for everything you could possibly say to me (to avoid buying), then I have virtually removed you from the scene. If, however, I set a stage for conversation and place *you* on that stage instead of my offer, and I look to *you* for direction, instead of trying to muscle you into a decision, then the entire experience will be unique and infinitely more enjoyable for you.

Forward motion tells me that I am not the center of the universe. Forward motion positions me as the salesperson at your elbow, and you as the buyer are glad to have me there. For thousands of years, sales people have been under the impression that the more they tell a potential customer about their product, the more interested the potential customer will become. If the price is constantly negotiated, the prospect cannot find a reason (or muster an ability) to say "no."

Think of the street markets you visit where people come from all over to proffer their goods, each one talking louder and faster than the next salesperson—all of them working to wear you down, to get you to surrender and hand over some money for their goods.

Another traditional technique for sales people is to never take "no" for an answer. I don't endorse this method, and in Chapter 3 I'll debunk this idea by showing you how you can take control of your sales through other techniques. Approaching any business prospect this way only leads to alienation of that prospect. And you'll continually be searching for more prospects under the false idea that it's all a part of the sales game. It's not.

This book is not about how to play the sales game. As I said before, this book is about how you can achieve a higher level of success in sales by reshaping your selling techniques and learning how to manage conversations in a forward motion.

Moving Conversations Forward

Selling occurs in traditional and non-traditional environments: over the phone, face-to-face, using conferencing tools, etc. This book will discuss the differences and subtle nuances of phone, face-to-face, video and audio selling. Some professionals consider these different forms of selling to be separate professions. But one thing remains true: Selling always involves moving conversations forward. How? Because *nothing happens until somebody sells something*, and this requires that a conversation moves from point A to point B and beyond.

Current technology—voice mail, e-mail, video conferencing, faxing, etc.—allows conversations to be made easier. But this comes with a price: Easier methods of communicating make for easier methods to avoid conversation or make conversation less inviting. Sending cold e-mails out, for example, may be the more efficient and less time-consuming way to communicate your message to a slew of potential customers, but this method won't connect you to those potential customers in a personal, human fashion.

Knowing how to use technology effectively, in conjunction with your personal connections, will make you a better—more successful—salesperson.

In This Book

My sales experience spans a variety of products in different geographical markets, from the East Coast to the West Coast of the U.S. But it doesn't matter whether you're trying to sell something in Dubuque, Iowa, Las Vegas or New York City; and it doesn't matter what you're trying to sell, whether it's local telephone service, commercial real estate or private club memberships. The concepts remain the same. The language involved remains the same. And the goal remains the same: to make those human connections by keeping in mind the notion of forward movement in every step of a conversation.

If you make your potential customers the center of your attention, then you will sell well in the long run and feel good about it. You will learn that there is no voodoo, nor trickery involved. It's about making connections on a small scale in order to make a difference on a large scale. And you will be surprised by what, given the philosophy set forth in this book, will motivate you in the future to sell.

In this book you will find:

- A new approach to selling via the human connection.

- Skill-based answers to the ever-present *How*? (Explanations on what to do, and what *not* to do.)

- An explanation of the three essential life skills—the three things we must learn to do in order to ensure our own survival—that no one ever teaches us.

- Stories of sales professionals who attribute their success to this process.

- Checklists to help you remember key ideas and stay tuned in to your goals.

- Points of Impact: These are nine essential reminders that illustrate the concepts outlined.

- The Big M: Motivation.

Move the Sale Forward

Perhaps the hardest lesson to learn: asking for help when you'd rather figure things out for yourself. But by reading this book, you are asking for help. That help is what can allow you to grow and make positive changes in your selling techniques...and move forward.

Now, let's get to work!

CHAPTER 1: MAKING THE HUMAN CONNECTION

Before delving into the mechanics of selling and the how-to's of making a human connection, we must go over some basic vocabulary. Understanding these terms will allow you to create forward motion, engage others and become a successful seller. Some words will be familiar, but others will be new or have new definitions that don't necessarily follow traditional schemes.

In all, these terms will change the way you think and approach selling…as well as the results you get. Keep each of these terms in mind throughout this book, as each one relates to a specific overall concept or idea.

Closing Is Coming to an Agreement

Let's begin with what is often viewed as the end of a sale: *closing*. The traditional goal of selling is to close the deal—i.e., get the sale, sign the contract, receive payment, etc. Closing is an essential component to selling, but it cannot be the ultimate goal. It's too shortsighted, too finite and therefore far too limiting. The goal, by contrast, is to move the conversation forward.

The problem with traditional takes on selling is that closing becomes too much a focus of the process. Traditional selling focuses on the end of the conversation—the closing. Conversations, however, are fluid and unpredictable. You should view each contact you have with a potential customer as a "piece" of an overall conversation conducted over time. The conversation starts, grows, ends and restarts. It can be unpredictable but that's what makes it thrilling.

If the goal is to close a conversation (i.e., get someone to be a customer), then the person will probably start to sense that. If you say, "Is this what you were looking for?" or "Are we ready to go to contract?" more than likely your potential customer will sense that you are trying to get to "yes." The person will know you're looking for a sale.

The goal, in making *human connections*, is to bring someone to an agreement with you in conversation. You want the other person to play as great a role in the next step of the conversation, which can mean the close of the sale, as you have.

Avoid statements like:

- "I'll call you next week."

- "Why don't we get together?"

- "I'd like to come to your office, so we can show you how we can blah blah blah…"

Some readers will cringe at these statements because lots of sellers use these as tools to "get the meeting." If you abandon these types of questions and statements, however, you will achieve a true human connection. You won't get a good response unless you rethink how to approach the closing. This brings us to the first Point of Impact:

☞ **Point of Impact #1:** When a potential customer hears an idea come out of your mouth, he hears an opinion. When he hears it come out of his own mouth, he hears facts or great ideas.

Alternatives to these statements and questions would be:

1) "When should we talk again?"

2) "How would you feel about us getting together to talk about this?"

3) "What do you think our next step should be?"

In traditional selling, we're urged to "close for the appointment," then "close for the order." Under this approach, there's virtually no allowance for any input from the potential customer. Any input from the prospect is viewed as troubling, inconvenient and subversive to the ultimate goal: getting the deal.

Sellers are sometimes equipped with false ideas about buyers (i.e., potential customers). These false ideas range from vapid statements like "buyers are liars" to "if they object, make sure you have a good, rehearsed comeback."

Statements like these are built on an assumption that the prospect—who you ultimately want as a customer—is the enemy. Worse, you're in a battle of wits and verbiage with them, hoping to wear them down, reduce their resistance, and get them to do what you want. No wonder people are reluctant to engage in conversation with a salesperson.

The buying public has been conditioned to believe that sales people are fast-talking, silver-tongued wizards to be wary of. Do you like to buy stuff? Of course you do.

But do you like to be sold? Probably not. No one likes to be sold, but it's a wonderful experience to buy stuff for ourselves, friends and family.

The sales approach, the reinvention of professional selling, rejects old ideas about buyers and focuses on conversations, emotions and expectations. It's not about closing the deal, but rather making the human connection.

Move the Sale Forward

> It's better to end a conversation with a prospect not buying, yet willing to speak to you again, than to bring a conversation to a close with a definitive ending to the potential relationship.

Your sense of self worth and your long-term career goals are better served by having the client/prospect's ear and not necessarily the sale. To forfeit the sale for the sake of the human connection is key. It allows for a possible sale in the future and does not disqualify the prospect as a buyer forever.

As I wrote in the introduction, the alternative to traditional selling is more realistic, sensible and fun. You'll feel better about saying "thank you" or "sorry to take your time" at the close of a conversation than saying something self-serving and never talking to that person again.

When you view closing as coming to an agreement, your focus is on what next step the potential customer would like to take with you. This creates a sense of cooperation and reduces the "I am being sold" emotional experience on the part of the buyer.

Put the prospect in a position of power and control, and thereby create a sense of comfort within the confines of your multiple conversations. This gets the prospect familiar with you, which in turn creates a greater understanding between the buyer and seller. Familiarity does not breed contempt; familiarity breeds understanding, and you want to understand your prospects. You want to connect with them. You want them to do the same.

Once a potential customer becomes familiar with you and understands you, you become less like a salesperson and more like someone he or she will turn to for help.

Remember: If you're trying to sell something that will help potential customers save or make money then, as intelligent decision makers, those potential customers will want to learn about it. But potential customers will first want to learn about you—without you trying to close them (i.e., get them to buy) the first time you get them on the phone.

By definition, a *decision maker* is someone who has the authority and responsibility to buy. To expand this traditional definition of the word, it's best to see a decision maker as anyone between the seller and seller's goals. So, in this sense, a decision maker can be a top-level executive at a major corporation or a receptionist answering the phone.

If you are an entrepreneur and own your own company, you have the authority and responsibility to buy anything for your company. This also makes you *qualified* to make decisions. The concept of *qualify* also relates to companies; you want to sell to qualified companies, those you target as potential customers.

All too often, sellers focus so intently on their desire or need to get the sale that they don't go one step farther and qualify companies before they get them on the phone. If you're going to spend a morning cold calling, you'll want to be sure to target your calls specifically.

> Qualify means to meet specific criteria. The more specific your criteria for potential clients, the clearer your path to cold calling and establishing a relationship that will get you a sale.

Move the Sale Forward

With an understanding of what *qualifying* means, it follows that in order for a prospect to qualify, the prospect first must meet specific criteria.

Examples of criteria for potential prospects include:

- Size of a company;

- Processes or raw materials they use; and

- Classification in a vertical market.

Other criteria can be added to this list, but every prospect will follow a different set of rules depending on the given industry or market. When you start to get a sense of whether a prospect qualifies as a potential customer, you must answer this question: *What is it that you sell?*

You may mentally answer with one or more of the following: service, products, experience or solutions. Perhaps you sell a combination of these things. No matter what you sell, one thing is certain: every seller sells *value*.

Remember: We truly sell value, regardless of what is on our pricelist or Web site. The value of what we sell is not determined by how difficult it is to produce or deliver. It's not determined by the competition's shortcomings. It's determined by the buyer, based on their own criteria. Buyers determine value, because they are the ones who write the checks for our product or service.

It's a great goal to do business with the top 25 companies in a specific industry. To get those 25, set some criteria and then find 50 companies that might also fit the criteria. As you disqualify certain members of this group over time, you boil the overall group down to the 20 or 25 you'll actually pursue.

Keep in mind that whether you believe that what you have to offer will be useful to prospects does *not* mean they will agree with you.

Enthusiasm is powerful, but as you'll see while working through the sales process, it becomes easier to identify potential long-term clients by being patient, walking them through a discovery process, and ultimately having them decide to do business with us, as opposed to our being focused on convincing them.

Traditional Thinking

Emotions run high in the business of sales (later we'll see how emotions dictate sales). As sellers, we get carried away because we feel that an appointment must logically lead to gaining a new client. Too often this is not the case.

An appointment simply means that we've achieved the next step in the conversation. So the traditional salesperson arrives to the appointment, makes a one-sided presentation, asks for the order, gets a non-committal response and talks himself into spinning the result into some success story, regardless of what actually happens after the appointment.

Now let's look at an alternative to this scenario. One's goal, in closing, should be to *gain an agreement*. This will, in turn, allow you to move the conversation forward. You can do this by asking one of these questions:

- "I can be there on Tuesday, how does that work for you?"

- "We can offer you 'A or B' or 'A & B.' Which would you prefer?"

- "How about I come in and tell you all that we do?"

Move the Sale Forward

But you don't want to make these suggestions too early in the conversation, without learning anything about the prospect. If you do, you may come across as presumptive and pushing an offer. Your offer then looks like a solution regardless of what the prospect needs and desires, or what interests him. This is not a conversation. This is duck hunting with a machine gun, without any specific duck in mind.

By disregarding any interests or needs on the part of the potential buyer, you are pointing an automatic weapon in any direction you feel is appropriate and squeezing off rounds. You keep changing the direction you are pointing the barrel in (changing your target buyers), until you finally hit something. In this manner, you forget about accuracy, specificity, and making a long-lasting positive impact. Even though you might hit a target eventually and count it as a win for you that day, it won't make you successful over the long haul.

Let's take another example, this time in the trenches of a used car lot. Assume that you are looking for a quality used car and that you have the money to buy one. Imagine that a person walks up to you the millisecond your toe hits the property line of the car lot.

"How you doing?" the beaming salesman asks. Up to that moment, you were fine, but now you are edgy, uncomfortable and you feel threatened. And the seller has not said another word.

As a professional seller, you know that your potential customers can sense when you're trying to sell them something—even if it's not a used car. But the scenario brings two things into view: emotions and instinct. Buyers (and sellers) have instincts and emotions that affect how they operate in certain situations.

If I try to sell you something, you can tell I am trying to sell it to you, even if I don't actually say: "Are you going to buy this from me?" Most people have the ability to sense when something is being sold.

Taking this fact a step further, it's important to note that, as a salesperson, you must not view others as different from you if you want to persuade them to buy. Just as you're not sitting at a desk waiting for people to call you, potential buyers aren't sitting at their desks waiting for your call just so they can reject you.

> Sellers and potential buyers carry sets of emotions and instincts that affect how they react in situations. But underneath, these different people are very much alike in character. Never view a potential buyer as being very different from you. View him as someone whose goals, wants, needs and distractions are similar to yours.

Making the human connection will only occur when you acknowledge that people overall are alike and that you have to practice a specific approach for gaining their trust. This happens more easily—for both parties—when you find a way to balance your approach between being aggressive and continuing to be proactive.

If you simply make a connection with the person who initially picks up the phone or is at the front desk when you walk in, then you can walk away—before closing a sale—at least satisfied that you have begun one more conversation.

All too often, the pressure to make the deal, gain the order or the appointment leads sellers to pick up the phone and try to make something happen. That pressure can be overwhelming. Remember that a good seller doesn't let the pressure to reach a sale affect how he or she approaches potential buyers. Maintaining connections with people—through emotion and intuition—is what gets results.

Replacing *I* with *You*

It's human nature to shy away from someone who forces you to do anything. If you try too hard to make a specific thing happen, or get someone to go down a road with you, you often won't be able to make that thing happen because you'll unknowingly sabotage or spook the other person out of going down that road with you. Although your intentions may be good, the actual perception from the other person is negative.

In our language, one word begins more sentences than any other: "I." Our challenge, and the key to making a human connection, is to replace "I" in our conversations with three words that people love to hear second to their own name: "you"; "we"; and "us." These words sound inclusive and are more pleasant to the ear.

The more you use the word "I" when you're talking to people, the more they feel as though you are talking at them instead of *with* them.

Most people are self-centered. This doesn't mean they're necessarily selfish or egotistical. It means they see the outside world only from their own perspective. To their minds, they are the center of the universe. Everything that happens can only be understood in relation to how it affects them. If you're talking to me and begin every sentence with "I," by the time you reach the third "I," you've lost my interest in what you have to say.

But, if you work toward making a human connection with me, you set yourself apart from the greater selling community. Now you stand out and open the door to reaching a sale.

Remember: Closing happens more often, and more naturally, when the conversation is about the *prospect's* idea and not the seller's.

We can't ignore the fact that closing is often viewed as an indicator of a job well done by the salesperson. It also (incorrectly) is viewed as happening as a result of the salesperson's mastery of the situation (or worse: the customer). But, as I've mentioned before, closing should be about coming to an agreement. To that end, the more you can have the potential buyer (and even the co-worker, spouse, child, etc.) make a suggestion, the easier it will be for you to get things moving.

A Macro View of Conversations

My view of a selling conversation is more of a macro issue than a micro one. This book will not tell you what to say when someone gives you a specific response. Of course, there are tools for you to use, as well as specific questions and answers for you to keep in mind, but the overall picture we will present is one that you can draw from in every situation.

The various ways in which people can respond are infinite and there's no way to cover every potential scenario. You'll have more control over how you act than how a prospect acts. And, since you know that you cannot prepare a prospect—or yourself—for every eventuality, you must readjust your expectations.

You must allow some leeway in what you expect from your prospects, as well as from yourself.

Because people learn and respond to things in various ways—some being more visual when it comes to absorbing and reacting to information, while others prefer verbal channels—it's beneficial to know how a prospect will best respond to you. That way, you can adjust your conversation to meet a prospect along his specific path.

Try to mirror a prospect's language. For example, if someone talks using visual cues, orient your response visually. If someone talks about how things sound, you should use sound-focused language.

Keep in mind, however, that you don't want to change your approach so much that you lose your focus from connecting with people. Stop talking. Listen to what a prospect has to say, ask questions based on what he says and see what conclusion he comes to, and you'll feel an enormous sense of pressure leave you. In general, people like to talk and listen to themselves talk. Having the patience to listen to what prospects have to say will open their trust up to you.

This approach is contrary to the "do whatever it takes to get the sale" mentality. It's allowing you to talk *with* the prospect as opposed to *at* him or her. The more the deal is the prospect's or client's idea, the better the idea seems to the both of you.

> In addition to mirroring the way a prospect talks and responds to information, it's also important to mirror the speed of the conversation. If the prospect talks fast, speak a bit more quickly. If the prospect speaks slowly, slow down a bit.

Don't search your mind for the perfect mirror-image phraseology and language. This will wither your focus and make you someone you are not. You want people to buy from *you*, not an adjusted version of you.

Aim to find the balance in your conversation with prospects between making minor adjustments and being yourself through and through. As a result, the people you'll do business with will be people you enjoy, and they will more readily refer you to people they know because they either believe you are good at what you do (and their associated company will benefit), or they simply like you as a person.

Feeling Your Way to a Sale

Buying is an emotional act. People can try to make it cold and rational—and some early stages of decision-making may be like that. But, most of the time, the final choice between two products or among several vendors is based on emotions. How they feel about you, the process, the way you approach them, the timing and patience you exercise, how well you listen (if you listen at all) and other emotionally-charged issues affect whether or not they choose to buy from you. Try and think of a time you've made a decision that didn't involve an ounce of emotion…and it'll be hard to think of one.

To review:

- Closing does not equal closure, but rather coming to an agreement;

- We must have conversations that flow and respect both parties' emotions; and

- Sales do not occur because we want them to, but rather because the two parties involved find common ground.

See the following page for a picture that represents the building blocks to a conversation.

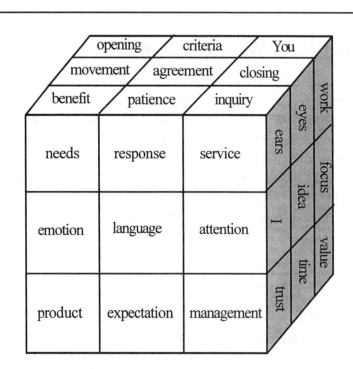

The Building Blocks to a Conversation

Many cubes come together in myriad ways to comprise a conversation, which is a forever-changing dynamic, mentally *and* emotionally. All the cubes are equally important as tools for moving a conversation forward. We could easily add more cubes and faces to those cubes, making bigger and longer conversations more complex in nature.

The Anatomy of a Conversation

Albert Einstein said: "Thinking is the most difficult endeavor that anyone could involve themselves in…and that is why so few people do." It's hard to disagree with this. After thinking, communicating with others through conversations is the next most difficult activity we engage in every day. It's putting our thinking into words; it's creating a channel of thought between two people. And it's as easy to lose focus in conversation as it is to lose focus in thought.

Why is conversation so difficult? Because two people have no idea what the other person will say from minute to minute. This is a *relational problem*, a disconnect between two lines of thinking. If you want to talk about dinner plans and someone else wants to talk about what movie you should see, you have a relational problem; you are not connected to the other person's issues and vice versa.

A conversation can be anything from an encounter with someone on the street, to a multi-year, ongoing relationship. All conversations have a beginning point, but may not have an obvious endpoint. We are all sensitive to whether or not someone else is listening to us. If you are in a conversation with someone who is not participating, you will know—and you probably won't like it.

In order to engage in conversation, you must always look for some common ground—some useful, solid bridge that spans the invisible gap between you and another. Try not to regard others as strangers, otherwise you'll always be on opposite sides of the bridge with people. Most people have an innate desire to connect with others—to build that bridge.

All conversations are made up of introduction, inquiry, response, listening, more response, an emotional tour and an end point. By *emotional tour* I mean that we mentally decide at each step of the conversation where we think we want the conversation to go:

- Is it okay for me to ask a more personal question?

- Should I reveal more of myself to this person?

Move the Sale Forward

- Does this person really think I am interesting?

- Is there any way I can get out of this conversation?

The time constraints and level of distraction of both people have a huge impact on the emotional tour. When you look for closure, you are actually looking more for a sense of clarity. Closure too often indicates the end of something. When a situation is clouded in mystery, the people involved certainly want clarity or *closure*. They *want to know what happened*.

Often, when you insist on closure during long conversations, you're looking for the other person to reach a decision and stay there. Or the desire is overwhelming to influence their decision, and thereby produce the result of an agreement. So be clear and don't look for closure in too many conversations.

On a vacation in Europe, my wife and I encountered a couple we hoped to see again. Classifying them as friends would be presumptive, since we may never see them again. But our encounters were certainly conversations that once begun we wanted to continue. I let this be known by subtly pointing out that our conversation was veering toward the end: "It was really good to meet you; too bad we don't live closer to one another." This is good to do with prospects in your business as well.

When a conversation comes close to its endpoint, point it out by giving the other person the freedom (and relief) to continue or break off as he or she sees fit. Allow the other person to decide whether or not to continue the conversation at a later date. If you say: "I'm glad we had the chance to talk," you open the door for the other person to suggest engaging in another conversation at some point.

Think about a developing relationship you started a long time ago. One of the most interesting parts of it is probably the time *between* conversations. Maybe you spent a tremendous amount of time on the phone with this person. Maybe you tried to come up with excuses to run into them in public places. But what is intriguing is wondering how the next conversation would start, and would the emotional tour continue?

Selling is, in a way, a romantic endeavor. You're looking for a deeper emotional tour. You're looking for people to invite you to return and continue the conversation. This creates forward motion and creates an emotional tour at a new level.

We've already touched upon the notion that people buy things based on emotion. People will buy from you because they feel that they are making a good decision, or they trust you, or because they think *not* buying from you would cause them to miss out on something. In the beginning, middle and end, they buy because they believe that they *should*.

A mistake traditional sellers make is that they want to expose and explore fear and loss. For example, some sellers feel the need to tell a buyer: "This is something that other companies are doing, and they're saving a ton of money; are you losing money by not doing this?"

But would you like someone to point out to you what you fear or what you might lose?

"Find their pain" is a popular sales mantra. A seller needs to think about what potentially pains his/her prospects. Did the buyer get a product or service of lower quality or at a higher price? If so, buying from you in the future relieves his or her pain. Did the buyer use a vendor who's not financially stable and as a result, is unable to receive the product or service on a timely basis? Then buying from you would prevent that from ever happening again. It would relieve the hassle. You can know a prospect's pain or what he needs to forward his business, but you don't necessarily have to point it out through scare tactics.

The people you interact with, or sell to all decide regularly—almost minute by minute—whether or not to buy from you. They decide to engage in forward motion because they feel as though it will be in their best interest. They decide to engage in forward motion with you because you are the one they feel most comfortable bringing on an emotional tour.

Move the Sale Forward

And that space, the ground you walk on over the course of that journey is as thin and fragile as pond ice. Be careful never to assume that because you have established a relationship that it will maintain itself through regular interaction.

> **People are busy living their lives in the space between emotional experiences—conversations—with you.**

When I manage my expectations, I create an environment where I am free to make a mistake. I am free to be creative. I am free from the pressure of remembering a set of "million dollar lines." The only people to make a million dollars from delivering a specific set of lines are actors.

Actors work according to a script. There are no surprises and they are only required to improvise in certain situations. Sales people, on the other hand, are required to improvise in every conversation. Even though I've presented 10-second descriptions of products and services I've sold over the last 18 years thousands of times, I still can't predict what the person on the receiving end will say.

Of course, I have an idea of what people will say, and I do get similar responses over and over again, but when I discovered the freedom and excitement that came with not trying to be prepared for every possible answer, sales became much more intriguing, fun and rewarding to me. I had fun responding to people naturally and without fabricated rules.

I remember the first time I cold-called an employment agency prospect in Southern California. I was working at home then (starting a business) and I put tremendous thought into my opening statement. I happened to get the decision maker on the phone, and said: "My name is John Klymshyn and I teach sales people how to operate at their absolute top level of skill and performance. How important is that to you?"

The decision maker couldn't just hang up the phone at this point. I had him in conversation with me from the start and I pushed it forward from there with an idea of what I wanted to get out of it. Part of the emotional tour that adds color, heightens the experience and can be difficult to implement is *expectation management*. Each of us enters into a sales conversation—in fact, every conversation—with certain expectations. I knew what I wanted to get out of my call to the employment agency from the beginning.

When I was young and I wanted something from my father, I would preface my inquiries with: "Are you in a good mood?" My Dad was a pretty happy-go-lucky guy, but if he was not in what I perceived to be a good mood, my expectations regarding his answers were somewhat pessimistic. I wanted to catch him at the right time to ask if I could go to a movie or have some money or invite some friends out on the boat that weekend.

I hated when I desperately wanted something, and the only thing between me and that something was whether or not Dad was in a good mood. Of course, with the perspective of years, I could see that his mood was not the issue. It was an issue of whether I was in good favor with Dad. Had I done my homework? Chores? Had anything he asked me to do slipped my mind? If so, it would be the first thing he asked me. If I had covered all of my bases, and Dad was in a good mood, I could expect a positive response. I learned how to manage my inquires and what to expect from my father.

The same goes for selling: *You need to learn how to manage your expectations and those of your prospects.*

I have planned phone calls with people, at specific times, on specific dates. When I called and they were not there, I had a choice. Do I get angry, impatient or lose sight of the fact that they have other things to do besides buy from me? Or do I take it as part of the process and build emotional equity with that person by never mentioning the fact that they did not do, say or act in a way that I expected?

Move the Sale Forward

I respect the prospect and work toward taking the next step in the conversation.

When people realize they have stood me up and I am patient and gracious, it brings me a huge step farther down the path of moving conversations forward. I can expect a connection to remain if I am patient and have respect for their busy lives.

The emotional situation I experienced as a child with my father applies to us as adults, particularly to our sales conversations. It's hard for sales people to find patience and stamina over a long conversation that doesn't turn a profit quickly. Sales people are paid to bring in business, so falling short of making a quota affects us in ways others might not understand. Someone who receives a regular, unwavering paycheck every week will have a hard time identifying with the fact that we sales people are successful only when we have closed more deals than have been expected of us.

So, with that kind of pressure, we tend to have a hard time with expectation management. We need to *manage* expectations, and not hang all of our personal worth on closing the deal. We must expect unexpected things to happen in every transaction. We must be willing to compromise and accept flexibility.

> Expectation management means you expect certain things to happen. You expect people to have lives, to be called away, to have things pop up on their desk unexpectedly—because you have similar situations all the time. The key is to manage that expectation so you don't put total control over your emotions in the hands of a decision maker, prospect or client.

The Human Connection

Another aspect to expectation management is *fine distinctions*. There are very fine distinctions between a closed deal and an ongoing negotiation. An ongoing negotiation still has things up for grabs. We have not reached any finality. We have not agreed on specifics that indicate to both parties that money will change hands.

Sales people—due to the challenge of the position and profession, the stress and the difficulty of creating transactions—begin to assume that a sale is closed long before it actually is. "Long before" does not mean minutes or days, but degrees of separation between the buyer and the seller.

The distinction is that subtle sign, word or signature that indicates to you that your prospect wants to become a customer. Don't think about your clients as people who are excited about buying from you. View them as people who are excited about what you offer.

The more you focus the conversation, your attention and the emotional tour on who they are, what they want, and whether or not what you offer will be of use to them, the more you can relax.

There is a big difference between bullying through a receptionist or executive assistant and making a human connection with that person.

You want to show that you are human, unique, involved, patient, respectful and professional. You do this through conversation, letting them discover these qualities in you. This is making human connections.

The human connection means connecting with people on a level that gains their trust and willingness to listen to you. It also means respecting people's time and acknowledging the fact that not everyone you call will be able to drop everything and hear you out.

> Do business with the people with whom you've connected. Approach people—not companies. Simply put, the human connection means connecting with other humans. The deals you close and the checks you cash will be the reward of your making those human connections.

You probably know who holds the money bags when it comes to potential customers. Don't foolishly try to wrestle control from those people without making those human connections. If you forfeit the connection, you sabotage the relationship and your prospect will only see you as another vendor, instead of a unique human to discover.

We pointed out earlier that a *decision maker* is someone who has the authority and responsibility to decide the next step. Most importantly, a *qualified* prospect is a person who meets your specific criteria for a client or customer. Notice that a qualified person isn't necessarily the one who decides to buy. Anyone with authority and responsibility to decide the next step in your selling conversation is seen as a decision maker. This could mean a secretary, a personal assistant, a spouse…even a child who happens to pick up the phone.

Don't Overlook Anyone

Some people have shared with me their perception of receptionists and secretaries and the monikers attached to these people (e.g., Gatekeeper and Goalie). With these mental images, how can people possibly approach these folks on a regular basis with the right frame of mind? If you view someone as solely an impediment to your goal, then you cannot help but approach that person with negative emotions.

Conversely, if you view that person as a decision maker, then you have a new level of respect for him/her; and he/she will have a greater desire to connect with you. In selling in the business-to-business environment, the more people you make a human connection with in each company, the better off you are. The turnover rate in companies makes it essential for you to make connections throughout a client's firm.

Keep two things in mind:

1) If your key contact leaves the company, you may be able to continue a selling/buying relationship with the company; and

2) If your key contact leaves the company, he or she may move to a decision-making capacity in another firm, and possibly provide you with a new client company.

In the coming chapters, we will outline the elements of making human connections in conversation. These include:

1) Listening;

2) Asking open-ended killer questions;

3) Gaining agreement;

4) Moving conversations forward;

5) Acknowledging the three essential life skills; and

6) Identifying emotional triggers.

There's a difference between listening to what someone is saying and waiting for him/her to finish talking so you can begin to make your point. Four essential qualities to have for conversations include:

- Skill;

- Habit;

- Persistence; and

- Humor.

Skill: Something that is learned (as opposed to a talent, which you are born with). You can learn to make human connections through practice, at which point it becomes a skill.

Habit: Something you do regularly, reliably and consistently. You will make a habit of your new approach to selling.

Persistence: The act of going on resolutely. You must have persistence in your selling methods, focusing on what *can* happen instead of why something should not happen

Humor: A good temperament. You must have the ability to take your work and your goals seriously…but not to take yourself too seriously.

While it's important to never lose your sense of humor, it's also key to never lose your sense of *human*. You can't be the perfect parent, spouse, speaker and seller, but if you can point out your mistakes, learn from them and perhaps laugh at them, then you'll be a better person overall.

So the human connection can only occur when you stop trying to come up with all of the answers and find out during the emotional tour what the prospect thinks, wants and how he would like to proceed.

Using the Phone to Make the Connection

There are significant differences between selling over the phone and selling face to face. Commercial real estate brokers, for example, who identify and negotiate lease agreements with corporate tenants and represent parties in the purchase or sale of commercial buildings, find it almost impossible to complete their transactions over the phone.

Your product or service may be one that does actually get introduced, qualified and decided upon over the phone (e.g., phone service, a magazine subscription or office supplies). Using the phone as a tool, however, applies to both situations.

The telephone is the single most powerful business machine ever invented. It requires both parties to be completely involved. It requires the person placing the call to be alert and responsive, without being distracted by what is going on near or around them. It requires immediate decision-making *on both sides* because it's conversation without the distraction of eye contact, movement or gestures.

Selling over the phone is, in some ways, more difficult to maintain than face-to-face selling, simply due to the lack of "recovery time," or the time it takes to reflect on what someone else has said. When a salesperson visits a prospect in person, there's an opportunity to decompress and re-evaluate the end of a conversation before moving on to the next. Whether traveling by car, foot or train, the face-to-face seller has time to breathe, think, evaluate and refocus.

On the other hand, when selling over the phone, the opposite is true. The good news is, that when we sell over the phone, we have an opportunity to build a momentum that is unavailable to the face-to-face seller. After I hang up with you, I can begin dialing the next number immediately. I can take the good feeling of a forward-motion conversation with prospect A and use that emotional energy as fuel for my conversation with prospect B.

When we experience a positive step, we get an emotional charge. When we complete a transaction, we feel almost invincible. The challenge is to put that good juice to work as soon as possible. Record your voice the next time you close a deal. Make sure you talk about your product but allow time for your prospect to contribute to the conversation.

Move the Sale Forward

Professional phone selling begins with developing and honing the skill of cold calling. Some will tell you that cold calling over the phone is a nightmare. It is immensely difficult. It can take your breath, motivation and self-confidence away in one fell swoop. All of these things are true, and that is exactly why so few people actually become good at it.

People who answer phones at most places of business are trained to ascertain facts from callers prior to dispatching the call. There are three specific things they want to know when they receive a cold call: *who?*, *what?* and *why?* Good cold callers know what these three things are and they know how to respond to these questions. Amazingly, this is where many professional sellers lose their rhythm because they simply do not prepare or are unwilling to answer these questions.

The three screener questions are:

1) What is your name?

2) What company are you with?

3) Why are you calling?

Because the selling process is more about questions than it is about powerful statements or the delivery of verbal brochures, traditional selling tries to skirt these questions with tricks and techniques. I have found, however, that if we answer these three questions up front, we have a better chance of finding out what we want to know (i.e., are they a potential buyer). We also have a better chance of finding out if we will be able to create and enjoy forward motion.

This brings us to our second Point of Impact:

☞ **Point of Impact #2:** The first person to ask three questions in a row has taken control of the conversation.

46

If you pull out of your driveway every morning at the exact same time, and run into traffic and a series of red lights, you have some choices:

- Accept the fact that traffic and red lights will interrupt your drive; or

- Try a different approach.

You can try leaving a bit earlier, or a bit later, and see how your results vary. If you know that all screeners/gatekeepers/goalies are going to want the answers to those three questions, you simply turn the tables, try a different approach and seek a different result.

A Case in Point

Grubb & Ellis is a commercial real estate advisory firm with 45 locations in the U.S. and 2,700 sales representatives. Their function is to find, obtain and fill requirements for office space leases, industrial space leases, and land and building sales.

When the company first adopted ideas for making the business move forward, it faced specific challenges. Professionals in the company found it inconvenient to make cold calls. Many felt it was necessary, yet were intimidated by the process. At the same time, however, it was generally recognized that cold calling would be essential to any informed business development plan.

The company viewed training in this process as something that might best benefit their newer or rookie sellers because there's a general consensus among folks who have been selling for a while that they have either mastered or graduated beyond cold calling.

The management in Grubb & Ellis saw a pending shift in the market and wanted cold calling to be a priority in order to maintain a competitive edge. Over the course of about a year and a half, approximately 200 of their people at all levels of experience adopted the *move the conversation forward* approach to their selling toolkit.

Most important, however, was the fact that people who hadn't consistently cold called for a long time were energized to learn about the basic truths of making human connections. They revived their selling techniques by asking open-ended killer questions and focusing on the prospect—not the sale. This brought them greater success.

They also were enthusiastic about getting into the trenches again and applying the *20 Call Burst approach* (i.e., making a solid run of 20 calls to new and old prospects, a topic we'll discuss shortly). Income went up. Office attitudes soared. Fun at work—and at home—came back. Stress was reduced.

Warm calling—negotiation, quoting prices and other topics of conversation—should in no way hinder the relationship between the buyer and seller. Much of selling is done out of fear. Fear that a competitor will get the deal with the biggest client in town; and fear that the deal may not happen. This fear interferes with the clarity of thought required to stand our ground and see things through to fruition.

Eight Essentials to Professional Selling

Beginning in this chapter and continuing in sequential chapters, we'll outline the eight essential elements to professional selling.

These essential elements are:

1) Imagination;

2) Organization;

3) Discipline;

4) Enthusiasm;

5) Perspective;

6) Product Knowledge;

7) Strong Communication Skills; and

8) Clear Objectives.

The first element, *imagination*, is applicable to and a necessary part of selling over the phone or face to face due to the fact that people know when we are trying to sell them something. Most folks want to feel as though they are being listened to and truly heard. Human connections don't guarantee a sale, but they lighten the load of having to create occurrences (i.e., closed deals, appointments, etc.). Using imagination to make selling unique and fun is part of the seller's experience—and challenge. No matter your experience, you won't be able to know exactly who will buy from you in the next 30, 60 and 90 days, what quantity those folks will order or dollar amount they will spend. This reiterates the need to see *through* the transaction, as opposed to *to* the transaction. You need to see through the transaction in order to create and maintain the relationship beyond that specific experience of the client cutting you a check. And this requires some imagination.

If you deal with someone as if he has the potential to become a client, you manage your emotional investment more effectively (expectation management) and you have a better chance of maintaining yourself as an effective seller.

Using your imagination is a two-pronged step: you are using your imagination to see through conversations…and, you are using your imagination to approach your potential clients in a meaningful manner. You want to be able to see them enjoying the benefits of what you have to offer.

It takes a lot of imagination to see through conversations when they stall and there's a delay on the other end. Be patient and flexible. You need to be willing to stay with prospects through their decision-making process. They will decide whether or not to buy from you for their own reasons—not yours.

To best see through those conversations, you need to have a sense of how your offer will impact your prospect's business and overall value. You also have to have a sense of your own trust in your product or service. Strong sellers have confidence in what they sell to others, and they have a good sense of who they need to target and how to go about getting those sales.

Professional Phone Selling That Works

Over a six-month period, I had the opportunity to work closely with people located in three of the Grubb & Ellis offices in Washington D.C., Northern Virginia and Bethesda, Maryland. We took a step-by-step approach, based on these eight elements to professional selling, making human connections and moving conversations forward. Among the things management felt the local brokers needed to work on, cold calling was at the top of the list.

We worked through sample conversations and broke down the experiences many had had with key decision makers. At the time, Grubb & Ellis was competing in a tight market for customers. So they needed to get an edge.

According to Phil Meany, the regional managing director of the central Atlantic region:

> This process (i.e., breaking down conversations and making human connections) shows salespeople an enjoyable way to do something that most find distasteful (i.e., cold calling). This shows them a way to be disciplined, enjoy the process of getting to know people and continue a conversation that builds toward business. Most people feel much more comfortable when that is what they are accomplishing, instead of making a phone call, asking someone if they need space today, being told "no," and then moving on.

And, according to Meany, "It's about enjoying what you're doing and being recognized on the phone as someone who enjoys what he's doing."

Conclusion

This chapter opened the door to many topics that we'll cover more extensively in upcoming chapters. The most important concept to take away from this chapter is that of making human connections. Our definition of selling: Having people feel good about making a positive decision *to move the conversation forward*, with you. Your goal as a professional seller will be to establish human connections with every potential client or customer—no matter whether they buy from you today, tomorrow or never.

Move the Sale Forward

CHAPTER 2:
BUYING IS EMOTIONAL

With emotion playing such a large role in how we connect, converse and move forward, you need to train yourself to identify the emotion involved in statements, questions and responses. In the previous chapter we said how people buy based on emotion. People make decisions more on how they feel than what they think is logical; having a gut instinct to do something, for example, can be considered a reflex to an emotion.

What does this mean for the sales professional? A lot. Understanding emotions and how they work when it comes to conversations and selling will allow you to maximize your connections and overall success. If you don't know how emotions play out in the world of buying and selling, then you can't sell or make human connections effectively.

This chapter will look into the role of emotion and teach you how to use and respond to emotion. No matter how hard you try, you won't be able to axe emotion from your daily work. It's a part of the selling profession. You will, however, be able to see the concept of emotion as a tool for moving conversations—and selling—forward.

Maintaining Control

How do we get involved in (and maintain) an emotionally charged conversation while staying in *control* at the same time? Sounds like a paradox, and to some extent, it is. Frazzled emotions aren't usually conducive to maintaining control over anything. This question brings us to our next Point of Impact.

☞ **Point of Impact #3:** The best way to direct a conversation is to keep some kinds of emotion out of it, while using others to forward the conversation.

The challenge, then, is to reconcile our use of emotional triggers without getting emotionally involved. In other words, you need to use emotional triggers as tools for connecting with people—but not for getting so involved in a conversation that you lose focus and your ability to manage it.

If you have ever been in a relationship with another human being, at any time—for any amount of time—you have probably experienced conflict. When you became emotionally involved in resolving that conflict, you lost something—and not just your temper. I am referring to how we all lose perspective and sometimes control when we attempt to resolve conflict in which we have an emotional stake.

When I ask groups of sales people in meetings: "When we become emotionally involved in resolving conflict, what do we lose?" their answers range from the unexpected "your dignity" to the logical "perspective."

Many sales people say that the best way for them to close a deal is to act as if they don't care if the deal closes or not. There is some validity to that, and here's why:

> As soon as it becomes apparent to the buyer that you have a great emotional stake in the specific transaction, you lose your negotiating edge.

You lose your position of power. You lose your ability to direct the conversation. So, the goals for you as a seller are to:

- Direct the conversation;

- Be persuasive; and

- Be perceived as non-threatening.

You want to move the conversation to more important and longer-lasting issues than price and delivery. If you achieve these three goals, you should be able to move things as you wish.

You then can begin to lay the groundwork for a new level of the relationship. In addition, you now have a path to follow. This cannot happen until you have a sense of how the people you are talking to perceive their business, their position in the marketplace, what you do and whether there might be a fit for your service within their organization.

Let's look at a couple of questions designed to address what you should be thinking about when it comes to the buyer:

- What is the best way for you and your potential customer to determine how you can work together?; and

- What do they need to know about your company/market/environment to figure out if what you offer would be of use or value to them?

You need a way to pick up clear signs in a potential client's language. Search for common ground and try not to change your style of talking and become someone you're not. The most reliable ways to understand where a person is emotionally is to learn, listen for and respond to *emotional trigger words*. These words give you an indication as to where someone is emotionally at any given time. Everyone who speaks English uses these words.

Here are some quick examples of emotional trigger words: *like*, *want*, *feel*, *believe*, *understand*, *agree*, *enjoy*, *hope*, *love*. Some other examples would be: *think*, *agree* and *hope*. Emotional triggers are among the building blocks to conversations.

Rigid Flexibility

One concept applicable to selling is the rule of *rigid flexibility*. Sounds like an oxymoron, but you probably follow this rule more than you think. For example, when you go out shopping for a particular item you want, such as a car, and you have to go from store to store to get the item you want at the price you want to pay, there is an air of rigid flexibility at work.

You know what you want and you have a really good idea of where to get your new car, yet you are flexible enough to either change the color you want from red to silver, or the date you acquire it, or whether you're willing to wait for an upcoming sale to see if you might be able to get it for less. That's having a rigid flexibility.

Let's say you target a particular vertical market—such as the insurance industry—and, over the course of a week, people mention a business or classification of business to you that you had not pursued. You start looking at the insurance industry but end up talking to people in computer security, risk management or personal finance. Upon doing some research, you find that companies in this sub-vertical (or possibly horizontal) market could use what *you* offer and it may be a significant competitive advantage to them.

For example: I have sold to the employment and staffing industry for quite some time. At a convention in Florida, I met people who were also vendors to that industry. Their services were ones I was familiar with and I immediately recognized how the employment market could benefit from using their services. I also recognized how these other vendors could benefit from *my* business.

We all had something in common, we connected as people and I managed to pick up new clients—the vendors serving my target clients. That's rigid flexibility. I wanted to be rigid, in that the employment industry was my chosen vertical market. I was flexible in that companies who sold to the same market, in effect, could become customers of mine. Clearly defining who I wanted to call on helped me to make sure I was asking the right questions.

You shouldn't try to know (or pretend to know) everything about a company before you contact it and meet with people. You want to be conversant enough about things affecting its industry (and its vendor industries) so you can communicate easier. This will open new doors for you.

When you encounter people—no matter where or what you are trying to do—you can have certain goals (be rigid) but be open to new possibilities. Take the opportunity to listen for, and respond to, key words people use. This helps you to gain agreement and direct (read: *manage*) the conversation and create forward motion.

A salesperson must constantly evaluate and re-evaluate his or her performance.

It's always key to remember that if/then statements are not reliable. Don't think that if the prospect says _____ and you say_____, then you will get the sale. Selling does not work that way.

If, on the other hand, you are flexible with how a conversation goes and don't rely on rules or formats for getting responses, then you will have better, more meaningful exchanges. You will best be able to handle unexpected comments and get to new levels of communication with prospects.

The Limits of Perspective

One Sunday afternoon, my family and I joined friends for brunch. During the conversation, I off-handedly made a comment about reading material that I had found particularly dry.

"That's dry?" the friend responded. "I'm really into that kind of thing."

Of course, that comment stayed with me for the rest of he day. Had I insulted him? Was I insensitive? Was I now thinking about it too much?

As the conversation with myself over the course of the day continued, the myriad emotions I experienced influenced and impacted how I felt. I wondered if I should plan to bring the subject up again when I saw my friend again. I thought I could call him and clear the air. I thought a lot of things—including the question of *why was this so hard?*

When a conversation hits a bump in the road, our faces get hot and we make bad decisions. We dwell. We re-run the event. We wish it never happened that way. We feel in trouble and want to press rewind. But this anxiety can be too much.

What I have found is how powerful an apology or admission of guilt can be. When this type of situation happened again and I apologized, I encountered comments like:

"I never really thought about it, because it didn't strike me that way, but the fact that it concerns you means a lot to me."

This is a great result, but I'd rather achieve it without having gone through the emotional sweat to get there.

Help!

Maybe you're too young to remember the Beatles' movie and album with that title, but if you are interacting with people at any level, you'll find yourself in a position where you'll need some help. Those of us in sales need all the help we can get because there's no way to get the information we need by ourselves.

The Internet is a good research tool. It can point you in the direction of basic information. It's limited, however, as to how deep it can go because Web sites, search engines and portals are not designed to help you think through problems or answer questions that are not fact-based.

> We live in an age where we can virtually get all pertinent information (factual) regarding prospects before we ever call them. Do this whenever possible; many people have come to expect it.

The mistake sales people make, however, is that they overuse the Web and fail to make human connections. People think if information is on the Web, it must be accurate. If a company advertises itself on the Web, it must have a product or service that fills a need. The only way for me to get reliable details about a company—including whom to speak to and how to reach him or her—is by talking to one or two people within that company. Don't rely on the company's Web site alone to answer all of your questions. Be reluctant to establish a relationship over the Web using e-mail unless there is some existing connection, such as a referral, a mutual friend or something else.

> The professional seller needs help—help that goes beyond the Internet. That help comes from making human connections.

For example, I witnessed the following at an airport:

A man looking somewhat travel weary held his jacket under one arm, a newspaper under the other, a boarding pass in his hand. The pass was in a folder provided by an airline, but not the airline whose terminal we were in. He glanced from the folder to the gate number he was standing in front of and back to the folder. He banged the folder against his leg and appeared to be exasperated.

I looked beyond him, to notice a few other folks watching him. Business travelers may not stick together as much as we should but we certainly exchange knowing glances when we see that someone is lost.

This guy gave all the appearances of being lost, and we hesitated to see if he would work things out on his own or if one of us should intervene.

Finally, two of us stepped toward him at the same time, and the other business traveler asked: "Do you need help finding the right terminal?"

The first gentleman was surprised, then did the double-take of looking from the folder he carried to the general surroundings, and then back to the two of us flanking him like secret service agents.

He let out a slight laugh and said: "No, I just got off a plane a few minutes ago, and I'm waiting for someone to get off another—we are supposed to meet here. I wrote his gate info on my old ticket."

The idea that he needed help was an emotional experience the other business traveler and I were familiar with. We were wrong about the circumstances and whether or not we could help—but we both felt compelled to help the poor guy. We only got to the truth by talking to him.

Filling Needs Needlessly

Sales professionals are often stuck in the dated mode of "find a need and fill it."

If you're only looking for "needs," you'll never take the time to learn enough about other people to know what they like or how they feel about different things going on in their industry. If you engage them in conversation, you have a better chance of learning whether or not they believe there is a difference between you and your competitor.

You want to understand them, and you ensure the flow of that kind of information by avoiding *I*-centric (i.e., egocentric) statements, such as: "I understand what your company is facing."

You know what it's like when someone tries to tell you how you feel or view things. You hear sales-pitch mumbo jumbo. Let's get off this course! Let's use, listen for and respond to what they think, like, want or believe. You want to bring them into the conversation when it will comfortably and logically take the conversation to the next step.

> **You must view (and direct) conversations in both a logical and comfortable manner while moving things forward.**

This is where the mental gymnastics—and real excitement—begin. Assume that you say: "I think you will like what we offer." The emotional response to this statement will be much different than if you are asked what you offer, you explain it briefly and then ask, "How does that sound?" or "How do you think that can help your business?" or "How do you feel about what we have discussed so far?"

These questions are instrumental in achieving the goals we set in Chapter 1, which were to make human connections, create and maintain forward motion and to engage the other person—instead of being the driving force in the conversation.

When someone asks you what you think, feel or believe, the chances are very high that you will tell that person. Most of the people you sell to are like you in that regard.

 Remember: We're looking for conversations that flow— that are not easy or effortless—but challenge us and require our mental involvement.

When we limit ourselves with the marching orders "find a need and fill it," we have great intentions, but end up driving off the road at increasing speed due to an inability to turn the wheel when necessary.

If you take your sporty vehicle out onto a mountain road and have a clear, definite objective of getting to the top, it's essential that you be open and sensitive to the potential turns, obstacles, unexpected events and driving habits of others. You can't simply hit the gas and speed around the curves without regard to life or limb.

Maybe that's a dramatic example, but selling—maintaining conversations—requires us to understand and adopt rigid flexibility. We're also better off if we don't set too specific an objective for each conversation. Uncover and discover people/companies/groups who may have a need or interest in your service.

If you are focused solely on finding a need and filling it, you are presuming that if you do find someone with a need, then you must kick into an artificial convincing mode and get the person to buy.

Let's go back to the mountain road. Your goal may be to arrive at the top safely and sooner rather than later. In the meantime, there is probably a more immediate reason you are driving up this mountain road. You're driving up this mountain road because you enjoy the trip. The twists and turns require something more of you than driving to the local deli for a half-gallon of milk. You feel challenged. You are interested. You are looking forward to surprises—a beautiful view, another lunatic in a sporty vehicle (whose driving you can criticize) or just the joy of the fresh air and sunshine.

The point is not to get to the destination in as hurried and frantic a manner as possible. Although you are a driven person (no pun intended) you enjoy the journey.

The Common Sense Thread

We often sense expectation on the part of prospects when we contact them. You can sense that a prospect feels the need to make something happen or respond to you in a particular way. There's pressure that builds from the action of simply picking up the phone and calling a prospect.

When a prospect knows you're calling to move him through the process from prospect to customer, his heart rate increases and he feel a bit of pressure. The best connections are made when you don't try to trade on or increase that pressure by attempting to close the deal, get the appointment or squeeze them for a referral.

The fact that the person you're calling has agreed to speak to you puts his/her mind into high gear. The person feels a sense of urgency and a partial obligation to either tell you he/she won't buy from you, ask you to be more patient or figure out how you can work together.

Getting around this pressure successfully moves conversations forward. Do this by exercising patience and being gracious and understanding.

Understand that people have other issues, other fires burning, so don't try to make them feel guilty about putting you off or not making a hurried decision.

Deciding to call them does not guarantee that they will be able to neglect the flow and flutter of their day in order to totally focus on your call. If you can sense that they are not prepared or focused enough to give the conversation fair attention, ask for a better time to continue the conversation.

You don't need to know right now if they will buy from you. Don't stare at the phone and wonder if the potential is slipping away. As long as the prospect invites you back, remain optimistic.

It's better to be invited back to a conversation than to force yourself on someone and ask for permission to call back. Someone who gives you an invitation will be more willing to listen to you the next time you open the conversation.

Move the Sale Forward

In general, sales people are not renowned for their follow-up skills. If they tell prospects that they will call people back—and they actually do call people back—it makes an impression.

Tell prospects: "The goal is not to do something quickly, but to do something if and when the time is right for you."

When you deliver that line to people who seem interested, but sound incredibly scattered or distracted, they truly do not know how to react, except possibly to feel relief because you are not trying to close them. And, it follows that if you are associated with a reduction of stress, instead of an increase, your calls are taken (even returned) more often.

As a seller, you need to learn to live according to your potential buyer's calendar—not your own. You need to realize that your selling quota does not translate to the prospect's purchase quota.

Finding a need and filling that need reduces selling to a transactional discussion, a less than skill-based profession, and it increases the level of frustration on the part of the buyer.

When you're cold calling, stay focused on the specific conversation and how to make it more comfortable for the person on the other end. Put people at ease by stating up front why you are calling and by asking them a question or two. Don't pressure and, more importantly, don't take the fact that someone will answer a question or two as carte blanche to conduct a detailed interrogation.

You should just want to talk. Just talk! If you can get to that emotional space, you have a greater chance at a future emotional tour. Emotional tours have indicators, and those are our emotional trigger words.

Some examples:

➥ How would you *feel* about our talking again in the future?

➥ What do you *think* we should do next?

➥ Where would you *like* to see us go from here?

➥ What would you *like* to learn about us, before it would make sense to continue the conversation?

These four questions have served me well, and continue to serve me, because of two important issues:

• They focus on the other person; and

• They employ an emotional trigger word.

Look at these sentences and find the emotional trigger word. What else can you discern about these questions? Each of them adheres to a specific qualification standard—they are all open-ended questions.

Traditional selling has, for some time, asked us to use "open probes"; "open questions"; or "open-ended questions." In Chapter 8, we will cover in specific detail how to ask open-ended killer questions. At this stage of our conversation, let's lay the groundwork for building upon these ideas.

Open-ended questions are those that cannot be answered with a "yes" or "no."

For most people in a business setting, saying "no" is easy. It means less commitment and less expensive. It's safe. The probability of getting a "no" when you ask a yes/no question is high. Some have quoted as high as 90 percent.

That means, if you ask 100 yes/no questions, you will get a "yes" only 10 times.

In the grand scheme of things, and if you relied solely on statistics, that might be okay. Unfortunately, selling requires more detail—more information—than just "yes" or "no."

A Quick Exercise

Ask someone in the family or at the office: "You don't want to eat anything, do you?" and see what he or she says.

Not only will the person be confused by the irrelevance of the question and to what's on his or her mind at the time, but the person will probably be confused by the fact that he or she is not sure what you want.

Ask someone in the family for money. You can probably guess what the answer will be.

The point of these exercises is to show how easy it is to ask—and answer—closed-ended questions. If, on the other hand, you ask an open-ended question, you will find yourself having to pay more attention to the response, and how relevant it is to your original question. For example, ask someone: "What do you like most about your favorite sport?" Make sure you have some free time, because many people will all but chew your ear off with their answer.

Contrast that question to: "Do you like football?" You won't get a very lengthy reply in comparison to the previous question.

> When you make an emotional connection with people, it's not about them liking you or you liking them (although the power of that is huge); it's about you uncovering through conversation something that they like, enjoy, hope for, want, need, agree with, understand, love or need help with.

I once made a phone call to a potential customer who was referred to me. The person was kind enough to return my call and as our conversation took shape, I shared with her what sort of services I had offered to the person who referred me. She mentioned the fact that she was familiar with my name and reputation (good, good), that she was facing a challenge and that she was unsure if I could help.

By exercising tremendous self-control, I did not blurt out: "Of course I can help!" Instead, I asked: "What are you trying to accomplish?" I did not focus her attention on how many problems I had solved for others. I did not quote prices. I did not say anything beyond that simple question.

After she outlined the situation she said: "Does that sound like something you might be able to help with?" I was positioned firmly in the navigator's seat. After hearing her out, I began my response: "It sounds like I might."

Her next question: "Okay, how?" That's when I got to tell her about past experiences that were relevant to her situation. I explained how it worked and what some of the obvious results were. Then I asked: "How does something like that sound?"

Her response: "Sounds great. Send me what you just said, in writing, and we'll figure out what days to get started."

This is exactly how the sales conversation should work.

It was not my quest to get her to like me or think I was witty. My goal was to help her. She may get my material and decide that my product won't work for her, and that's okay. That's part of selling. The key is to be strong enough to know and openly admit when what you offer will *not* solve the problem of the prospect or customer.

If you succeed in selling your service or product to someone who really can't use it to his or her benefit, you will lose customers. It takes a lot of courage to turn someone away whom you know you can't help. Not serving the best interest of the customer, in order to notch up sales numbers, is a surefire way to lose people. It will always backfire.

Move the Sale Forward

You'll be surprised how much satisfaction you can get out of conversations with people that you'll never do business with. It's about making human connections—no matter what. And I make those connections by identifying, listening for, responding to and using emotional trigger words.

Remember: Emotional trigger words such as *think, want, hope, help, agree* and *understand* are the tools you can use to build relationships, generate new business and feel good about the process.

Looking Too Far Ahead

Sellers must remember not to lose sight of immediate obligations by looking too far into the future. If you want new business today, today is not the day to start working on generating that business; it's too late.

The sales cycle—from identifying a company as a potential customer to turning it into a realistic prospect and then into a customer or client—is one that requires constant attention. It's easy, however, to look down the road at the total length of the sales cycle and get antsy. A seller may feel as though his current movement is too slow, and get distracted by this.

If we had the opportunity, and went back in time to monitor the movement of the glaciers during the Ice Age, it wouldn't be as exciting as the Indianapolis 500. The movement was slow and not so easy to identify at any point in time. But the impact of the Ice Age on the world was huge. Continents moved; cultures developed; and at some point farther down the road, people started to communicate with one another. It took many small changes for the overall impact to be realized. It took many changes to equate to one large change.

The same holds true with selling; it's a profession that requires small activities if we're ever going to see long-term results. When we view the process as long and methodical, it is easy to push off specific directed activity for a day or so. That day or so turns into a week, and dangerously, turns into a month.

I've encountered many people in my career whose goal is to land that one special deal or find that one special client that makes them all the money they ever dreamed of. They search for these things because they are unwilling to put in the small daily efforts, which add up to one huge effort. They are, effectively, on a hunt for the pot of gold at the end of the rainbow.

They feel as though selling is about being in the right place at the right time. All they need is one special sale or client, which will allow them to spend their days at the country club while the rest of us sweat it out at the office every day.

 The easy sale, the big deal or monster account are, unfortunately, myths.

You may have heard of someone who negotiated a huge deal and as a result, became financially independent. What the news and grapevine fail to tell you, however, is that those people are few and far between.

Selling is about expectation management. It's about discipline. It's also about money…and accomplishment. Once you get a taste of that special sense of accomplishment, you want to do it again.

Long-term relationship building does not mean we should wait a long time to move the conversation forward. You need to be able to pick your prospects well, learn to invest your time and effort into each of them, fully aware that not all will respond to you in a way you'd like. If you work hard at maintaining conversations and seeking the beginnings of new ones, you will reach your sales goals.

As you evaluate a given day's activity—the decisions you make about who to approach, which market to learn more about, or what competitor you would like to rattle—beware of the classic *paralysis by analysis* syndrome. *Paralysis by analysis* is the situation where you spend so much time and energy thinking about what you should do, that the end of the day arrives and you have actually done nothing.

Take a risk and do something rather than be too cautious and accomplish nothing.

Until you take a step, you have no momentum in any direction. Selling is a non-stop treadmill. If you don't keep stepping forward, you are removed.

A Little Inspiration

In your try to plan well for the future and succeed in the long-term, you probably wonder about the *today* part of the equation. What can you do today to make those long-term goals happen? According to Og Mandino, author of *The Greatest Salesman In the World*, there are seven essential characteristics to a successful endeavor or successful person. The most basic is: I will act. I will take charge of today in whatever capacity I can and make the best of it. I will live this day to its fullest. I will dream and reminisce and visit a pleasant past with my eyes toward a wonderful future. The key requisite for both is a positive and productive *now*.[1]

In the grand scheme of things, this day may appear to be like any other. No great similarities or differences from any other day. But similar days add up to a lifetime, and subtle changes on a daily basis will make for a lifetime of action—and an evolution of change.

---

[1]*The Greatest Salesman in the World* by Og Mandino; Bantam Books, 1983.

Remember: We must act, today. This could mean doing something minor that is a stepping stone toward a greater, loftier goal. Everything you do should be going in the right direction: forward. Acting now makes your future more productive, enjoyable and stress-free. The idea is to create a compelling future for yourself by initiating action *today.*

SureWest

Ted Allegra is the Director of Sales for Roseville, California-based SureWest, an ILEC (Incumbent Local Exchange Carrier). SureWest is a diversified communications company with over 130,000 customers; it provides consumers and businesses with Internet, data, DSL, wireless and local telephone service. Annual revenues run around $155 million.

Allegra's job, when we met, was to manage sales, recruit sales people, retain top performers, increase the number of customers, the amount of revenue and the penetration and placement of services with those customers. In short, his job was to sell.

Before the company began to change the way it approached sales, it faced two things:

1) A lack of consistent, outward bound prospecting and business development; and

2) A team that lacked the necessary skills and tools to perform the sales function on a sustained, day in and day out basis.

SureWest didn't have a structured way for selling and generating new business. They needed to find a way to feel good about prospecting and generating business, as well as a way to be most effective for improving their bottom line. The human element of my approach made a difference. According to Allegra:

> We needed an approach that centered around the needs of the human touch or the human interaction. The center of the discussion with a customer does not have to do with "This is what we are selling today," but instead, "What true needs or opportunities exist in their business—now and in the future?" Knowing that the objective is to take the customer to a new level, not necessarily to a contract, is key.

I worked with Allegra's team and taught them how to take conversations to new levels.

We started by going over the mechanics of selling within the framework of the human connection. We worked with the company's sales people and management to train them how to utilize their time effectively, make those 20 Call Bursts and learn how to move conversations forward. The focus became moving conversations forward, rather than direct sales over the phone.

Allegra notes: "When you and the customer see that there is a benefit to the conversation, then you can move things forward. If you don't both feel the same, then the conversation is over."

Allegra felt a huge difference in the mood of his team once they learned the basics and were all on the same page when it came to selling tactics:

> If I walk around people's desks as they are on the phone, I will hear specific key phrases that are being used on individual calls. I hear the skills being applied. I guess the strongest sense I have about the long-term impact is that when I talk to my staff to ensure that they are on track, we now have a common language. We ask open-ended questions; we use key phrases that are complimentary to the business moving forward; and we spend just enough time on the phone to move it to the next step.

Allegra turned his selling team around by using the same tactics I explain in this book. "It has also helped us to have our folks focused on behavior, instead of mood or outside influences," Allegra adds.

This is exactly the point of this book. You can learn how to sell and sell well if you think of yourself as a person rather than a salesman. You are someone who behaves like everyone else, with moods and the need to maintain conversations throughout your day. If you approach sales with this mentality, you're well on your way to being a successful professional salesperson.

In Chapter 8, when we examine killer questions in detail, we'll return to SureWest and share with you some of the killer questions that helped change the company and helped improve its bottom line.

Conclusion

Knowing how emotions play in how people—even you—make decisions is key to your selling career. People will always buy based on emotion. People will always buy from someone they feel an emotional connection with, no matter how small. And people will always come back to buy more from someone that makes them feel comfortable, who takes their business seriously and who knows that an agreement will be mutually beneficial.

If there's one craft sellers hope to master, it's engaging others in sales conversations. It involves many things, starting with thinking about the buyer's goals rather than your own. It also takes some *imagination* and *organization*, two of our essential elements to selling professionally. In Chapter 3 we'll get into the details of this craft and come to learn how conversations are really 80 percent listening and 20 percent responding.

Move the Sale Forward

Chapter 3:
How to Engage Others in a Sales Conversation

As we move through the big and small issues regarding our approach to sales, it's essential that we lay a certain foundation. People need to understand each other by speaking the same language and using the same map. Think of the map as your key to moving conversations forward, which is synonymous with successful selling.

We've already defined many terms that can serve as points of reference on our map. Now, we'll go further by setting some standards—a legend, if you will—on this map to help us better navigate. It starts with those eight steps for selling professionally, which we started detailing in the first chapter. They are the tools for engaging others and involving others in your ideas.

Traditional sales philosophies address the question "How can I sell" by urging sales people to:

- Ask questions designed to get a "yes" response (i.e., "It's a nice day, isn't it?"; "Insurance is important isn't it?"; and "Do you want to buy an insurance policy today?"; and

- Never take "no" for an answer (which is a reliable ploy if you want to alienate your prospect).

These philosophies do not correctly address the question: *How can I learn to sell?* Based on experience, observation and testing in multiple markets at various dollar levels, the eight elements presented here have served me, my clients and my students well.

To put it simply, these eight elements are:

1) Imagination;

2) Organization;

3) Discipline;

4) Enthusiasm;

5) Perspective;

6) Product Knowledge;

7) Strong Communication Skills; and

8) Clear Objectives.

In this chapter, we'll review the first and discuss the second.

Imagination

Imagination may sound intimidating because the word makes many people expect creative genius. This isn't what we mean by *imagination*. In terms of selling, imagination means using your mind to foresee the movement of a conversation—to predict, problem-solve and see positively a potential cooperative outcome with another person, while at the same time engaging that person in conversation. It also means helping your prospect conjure positive images in his head, which isn't easy to do. Look deep into your creative side.

> Imagination means that you, as the seller, must be able to see through or beyond the transaction while engaging the prospect in conversation. You want to imagine your customers enjoying the benefits of what you sell.

When you think about your conversations with potential customers, picture good situations and solutions, as opposed to negative images of loss as a result of your not doing business together. Clear your mind of the distractions and issues of daily life—even business life. Concentrate on your customer and your products…and why they fit together.

Never assume that someone will say "no" before you've asked for a sale.

Never become so pessimistic that you can't focus on your customer.

Imagination asks you to look at the process of selling from a distanced point of view and manage it with a sense of wonder. Sellers get knee-deep emotionally in the process, instead of keeping the process and its outcomes at an arm's length. While managing your expectations, you want to establish a different conversation with the prospect than the one he has with your competitors. If you can set yourself apart from anyone else out there—selling anything—you have achieved a wonderful thing.

Since what you sell is *value*, you must engage your prospect with open-ended questions, which lead to more detailed and unique conversations than if you ask plain yes/no questions.

A few yes/no questions are:

- "Can I meet with you on Tuesday?"
- "Does that sound like something you would want to do?"
- "Is this a good time to talk?"
- "Did you do your homework?"

A few open-ended questions are:

- When would be a good time for us to meet?

- How does that sound to you?

- How is my timing?

- How is your homework coming along?

See the difference? The open-ended questions automatically engage others, getting them to use their minds in order to form answers (as opposed to responding reflexively with a "yes" or "no").

When we consider imagination, not only are we interested in picturing conversations in our head, but also setting a tone for every ensuing conversation.

We will discuss the building blocks for open-ended questions further in Chapter 8.

Difference Between Selling and Telling

Selling *is not telling, talking or convincing* and the difference between understanding how to sell and practicing the craft of selling has made a huge income difference for me and many of my students. Our definition of selling is: Having people feel good about making a positive decision *to move the conversation forward*, with you, today.

Sales has traditionally been populated by people who like to talk. There have been multiple stereotypes set in people's minds regarding this profession, (some grounded in reality) that a salesperson is pushy and overbearing. They achieve sales by talking people into purchases. These folks will tell you how good their product is. They will tell you that you need to act (decide to buy) fast, because another prospect is waiting, and if you hesitate, you will lose out.

Their mantra: "Keep talking until someone signs a contract."

Chapter 3: How to Engage Others in a Sales Conversation

Try taking yourself out of the process and work toward not being the center of the conversation. In the same way that you should replace *I* with *you*, *we* and *us*, you want to make some other changes in the standard selling lexicon. Sometimes it's more than replacing the word *I* with *you*; rather, it's the perspective of the entire sentence.

 **Use Instead:** *You*, *We* and *Us*. Or, find ways of shifting perspective, focusing on the potential customer.

Replace:
"I wanted to let you know…" and
"I have information that will be useful to you."

With:
"I'm calling to find out…" and
"What info could I provide that would be useful to you?"

Note that the second set of sentences still use the word *I*, but they focus on the potential customer—and not the seller and his product. Sales people in past generations who were referred to as "bag toters,"[1] were playing a numbers game every day. There was no pre-qualification. If your company had a front door, it would get knocked on by sales people. There was no sense of being able to forecast sales and sales weren't built on relationships with customers. This was an approach used by people who sold both to consumers and businesses. It's archaic today. We can

---

[1] These were folks who would tote a bag of samples around, and knock on every door, looking for the one person in a huge number that would buy from them. The level of sophistication of the sales technique was "Knock on every door—eventually someone will buy from you."

see that even then there was a need to employ imagination, because the first "no" could have been the end of the salesperson's selling day.

Being rejected is no fun at all.

I've been selling for almost two decades. When I don't have a full calendar, I cold call and the rejection still gets to me. The most reliable cure I've found is to mentally run through the reasons why someone should buy from me and I gather the courage to pick up the phone again.

Negative responses will naturally get you frustrated and kick you in the stomach. But that kick will make you keep going. You must accept that you will not engage and involve every person you speak to. You know that your prospects are being cold called by dozens of other people every day, trying to be sold on something else.

Think About the Buyer's Goals, Not Yours

When a salesperson cold calls a company, he or she must put aside the desire to find a need for this company to buy. The salesperson will be most effective and better received when he replaces that agenda with a curiosity about the company or person he is calling on.

You cannot transact business without qualification and determination of prices or fees. You cannot quote prices and fees without the prospects learning how the investment or purchase will help them. You cannot explain how the purchase will help them until you have at least a cursory conversation.

And you cannot have a cursory conversation without an introduction.

Working backwards gives us an outline of steps in the sales process. However, it does not inform us *how* to achieve each step. When people call you, for example, convinced that what they have to offer is going to be good for you, they don't involve you in that decision. They assume that you'd benefit from their product or service. Wouldn't you rather be part of deciding whether something is good for you or not, than be told it's a good idea? There's a way you, as a seller, can get the prospect to think what you offer is what he wants or needs.

When you call a prospect, you want to use your imagination to create a dialogue about *your prospect's* company, *your prospect's* situation and what *your prospect* thinks. Don't focus on your product and how advanced, affordable or useful it is. At least not at first.

Imagination means that you're not calling to try to create a transaction today. You're beginning—and hopefully forwarding—the discussion so that when the time is right for your prospect to consider what you offer, you'll be the first person she contacts.

As a salesperson, you must focus on creating transactions and on building relationships. You must also realize that the more dollars involved in the transactions you create, the higher the chances are that you'll be involved in a multi-step sales process.

 Remember: A seller must accept that the multi-step sales process requires patience, persistence and time. Selling also requires thinking about the *buyer's* goals, business and needs.

Practicing patience and focusing on the buyer can drive some fast-thinking, hardworking sales people crazy—especially those who want to make quick deals.

Using your imagination means not throwing numbers up in the air and wishing for those commission checks to come in automatically. If you're going to go about selling the right way, then you must have patience and foresight, as well as an appreciation for the process rather than just the end result.

Move the Sale Forward

Our next Point of Impact helps us manage our mindset.

☞ **Point of Impact #4:** The appropriate time to celebrate the sale is after the commission check clears your bank.

The whole point of imagination is to see the conversation and the subsequent potential sale from the long-term view. Too often, sales people celebrate the sale prematurely. They think that because they get an appointment, they have won a new client or will definitely achieve a transaction. This is like getting an interview for a job and automatically thinking that you're going to get an offer of employment.

Imagination's most dramatic application is in our mastering the mental discipline of seeing *through* the transaction, not just seeing *to* the transaction.

Unequivocally and without reservation, I believe that the transaction is the salesperson's nirvana. It's where we all want to go, as often as we possibly can.

We get frustrated, lose focus and, at worst, lose deals when we lose sight of how things really work. Quick action, without careful planning behind it, is often wasted. You need to see through the transaction—even if you'd rather focus on it.

Single-transaction business makes life difficult for the professional seller. Most want multiple transactions, preferably with the same buyer. There is a significant reduction in the amount of effort required to create second and third transactions with someone, because so much of what we work at has been achieved. In addition to (possibly more importantly than) gaining the transaction, is that we've earned the client's trust. And, they have proven their ability to buy.

Chapter 3: How to Engage Others in a Sales Conversation

We don't want someone to buy from us once and never again. Of the various sales people I've dealt with, and the various dollar amounts of their transactions. I have yet to encounter someone who's looking for one deal per customer. If that were the case, then all they would do all day is go out looking for new customers.

Prospecting for new customers is an integral part to the profession. But the ability to return to customers or clients who have bought from you before is wonderful; you hope that if they've bought from you once, they'll buy from you again and again.

· Seeing through the transaction means using your imagination to envision the customer enjoying the benefits of what you have to offer.

In order to imagine enjoying the benefits of what you offer, you must learn enough about your prospects to determine if there are any features or benefits that will enhance their lives, build their businesses or save them money. The benefits you see in your product or service are not as important as the benefits your prospects see in your product or service.

Remember our first Point of Impact: When someone hears something come out of your mouth, he hears an opinion. When he hears something come out of his own mouth, he hears facts or great ideas.

So, although you may love what you are selling, the ability to deliver a unique and uninterrupted speech that touts all of the good things about it does nothing for you. Find out from your prospect what your service will do for them.

The only way to find that out is by involving and engaging them in conversation, and making sure that the conversation is ruled by the 80/20 approach.

> **Pareto's Economic Principle, less formally called the 80/20 Rule, applies to many things. Eighty percent of the work is done by 20 percent of the people.**

Move the Sale Forward

Applying this concept to selling:

- Eighty percent of the sales are made by 20 percent of the sales people;

- Eighty percent of our job as sellers, communicators, etc. is *listening*; and

- Twenty percent of our job is *responding*.

Imagining your clients enjoying the benefits of what you offer removes a sense on their part that you're trying to grab them by the throat, wrestle them to the ground and take their money.

It replaces the preconception: "Here comes another salesperson." with: "I wonder if this will help me?" This is what we want going on in the minds of prospects. We want *them* to come to their own conclusions. We want *them* to invite us in for an appointment. We want *them* to ask prices or ask for proposals. We want *them* to suggest a tour of their facility or look at their current situation or their last attempt to solve a particular problem.

> **When we're invited to come alongside a prospect and look at an issue *with* them, our potential to win the business increases. The percentage of probability increases because they are looking for our input.**

One of the biggest challenges for you and your selling career will be to discipline yourself to *only answer the question asked*!

Cutting to the Chase

Early on, I was so thrilled that prospects would even engage in conversation with me by asking me anything, I would run off at the mouth—usually with things that had nothing to do with what they asked me. I saw their questions as open doors, through which I should drive a truckload of information.

The questions *are* open doors. But a truckload of information is more than most people want.

The emotional experience has not changed, but my level of discipline has. I still get excited when someone asks what I do, or how I do it, or even for whom; it's a big part of why I still sell…because it's fun!

But now I limit my answers by making them more focused, and more often than not I follow my answer with a question, which will get them talking again. This is the verbal editing that every salesperson—every businessperson—needs to practice.

I have, over the years, found answering or responding only to what is asked to be difficult, yet incredibly rewarding.

When you ask me for some references, I can tell you every customer I have ever done business with, or I can ask: "How many names would you like?"

When you ask me how long I have been with the company, I can give you my verbal resume, or I can answer the question with a number of years or months—without elaborating on anything else that's not relevant to the question you asked.

An analogy would be in a courtroom when a witness is asked a question, and he/she starts to feel they're not getting a chance to tell the whole story and they're warned to "answer the question being asked."

Verbal editing is not designed to withhold anything from anyone. It's a tool of efficiency as well as a safety measure. The more you can stay on topic with your prospect, the shorter your conversations will be because you get to the point. This shows respect for the prospect and his or her time.

Here's where the fun starts. Striving for responsiveness and efficiency puts us on a level of communication with prospects and customers that few (if any) other sales people get to. This level is achieved because we have learned to cut to the chase. We get to the meat of the discussion. We see the exciting stuff. We want to move the conversation forward.

> **Have you ever asked someone a simple question, and the response you got makes you sorry you asked? Think about the cliché of asking someone what time it is, and the person went into a detailed answer telling you how his watch was designed.**

Another traditional sales experience is when a neighborhood kid comes knocking on the door to sell you something for a fundraiser. The kid begins a prepared speech and within a minute you interrupt the kid and say: "Sure, I'll buy a (subscription, candy bar, etc.)."

The kid is dumbfounded. You've interrupted him and his training doesn't allow for this contingency. So the kid begins his entire speech again and you realize you must wait until the end. The kid needs to deliver his closing and ask for your order.

It may seem a bit of a stretch to apply this problem to professional sellers, but so much is going on in our minds during the selling conversation that we sometimes get disconnected from it and lose track of the ultimate goal: *Connecting with the person with whom we are speaking.*

This will not happen as the result of a prepared speech or script. It will not happen as the result of practicing every if/then scenario.

Remember: Imagination means we must look beyond the transaction to the long-term relationship. We must not celebrate the sale too early, because at any time the relationship, the requirements or the deal itself can change, or worse, implode.

Imagination leads us to the next element of selling professionally: *organization*.

Organization as a Tool

Organization is the tool that sales people need the most. Everything from spiral notebooks to the latest versions of a hand-held PDA (personal digital assistant) have been used, embraced or discarded by sales people in their attempt to stay organized.

Everyone has a different method of staying organized. Some need to write things down in their own handwriting. Others find typing or tape recording helpful. And many find the latest technology in personal organization (i.e., those Palm Pilots and Blackberries) useful for their day to day activities.

Sales people are more productive when they've taken the time to plan their day before starting. It's possible to show up at the office with a fair head of steam, jump into the fray and walk away at the end of the day with some results, but the people who are organized attain more consistent results. They have a sense of how they can continue on their path, have lower stress...and have more fun.

Organization is not restriction. Sales people like the freedom to work at their own pace, to solve problems and to avoid doing the same thing over and over. They can do all of these things, if they know where everything is their working day…is.

Organization is the responsibility that allows the freedom a career in sales can offer.

You'd get a variety of responses if you were to interview 10 sales people at random, and ask: "Why or how did you get into sales?" But among the answers you'd probably find something like: "I was looking for more freedom in my career." The paths to this profession would undoubtedly vary. If you were to ask the same group: "Why do you stay in sales?" Their top reasons would likely be one of these:

- Freedom;
- Thought/Mental Challenge; and/or
- Fun/Thrill/Risk.

Notice that big bucks or money is not on this list. Freedom comes up again and means a lot to sales people. Folks whose answers include money are the people getting the least out of the profession.

Having a lot of freedom, however, in one's career requires organization. Why? If you're not organized, you won't be most effective with all that freedom. You'll waste time in disorganization and miss out on focusing on your prospects and ultimately, your sales.

Try using software that helps manage your database and record specific activities. You can find software that merges with other programs, like a word processing program so you can type form letters (or even single letters) and have the information of the contact record imported into a document without having to cut and paste or re-type the information. It's worth spending some time playing with a few programs and seeing which ones work best for you.

> Find a software program to manage your database that is easy to use, is compatible with other programs (e.g., a word processing program) and that you feel works for your business. Make sure it reminds you or prompts you to make calls. And if, for whatever reason, you do not make a certain call on a certain day, the software can forward the action to the next business day so nothing falls through the cracks.

You can use software to track the current, past and planned future activities with each individual contact, as well as keep track of where you are in any given conversation with people. You'll know, for example, when the last conversation occurred with someone and what was discussed. There are dozens of these programs for sale in most office supply stores and at many sales-related Web site. Most work fine. The particular brand you choose is less important than the commitment you make—to yourself—to use it.

Software isn't the only organization tool you'll need. Some physical tools—things you touch and feel—can also help.

Headsets are an example. How do headsets make you organized? They help free you from the distraction of a phone handle. This, in turn, will make you more organized. You'll be generating outbound calls in specific groups (See Chapter 4 for the 20 Call Burst). With your headset on and your software program opened, you'll have quick access to all the information you need.

Three Questions for Organization

If someone is truly organized, it's a habit. And in order for you to get into the habit of being organized, answer the following questions:

Move the Sale Forward

- Who?;

- What?; and

- When?

Who? Every salesperson must have a sense, if not a confirmed list, of who—specifically—to call first, second and throughout the selling day. By choosing a vertical market, we identify specific qualifications that the companies or organizations we will call must adhere to.

If I ask sales people *who* they will sell to on a given day or who they potentially can sell to, and I hear, "I can sell to everyone," I am dismayed. The unfortunate fact is that if you feel as though you can sell to everyone, you are actually saying that you can sell to no one, because "everyone" is too vague. There is no listing for "everyone" in the phone book or on the Internet.

Whatever method you use to find people, companies or prospects, you must employ some criteria. You can't aim to make "everyone" a prospect. That's not defining your market.

The criteria questions I use are:

1) Who makes the decision to buy? and

2) Who influences that decision?

Once you define some qualifying criteria, then you can start to answer the question *Who?* On a daily basis, you must answer the question *Who?* in a specific sense.

Chapter 3: How to Engage Others in a Sales Conversation

What? This question is two-pronged. We want to know: a) What we want to talk to the "Who" about; and b) What do we want as a result of that conversation?

Each contact with a prospect should have, as its ultimate goal, one thing: to move the conversation forward. Newton's law of inertia applies as dramatically and reliably to sales as to any other application. This laws generally states that something at rest stays at rest, and something in motion remains in motion (unless, of course, a force is applied).

For example, every six weeks I print a hard copy of my database of prospects and clients. Even though I trust my software (and my backup procedures) to remind me who to call and when to call them, I don't completely trust my discipline in recording the information. My personal sales cycle—the period of time from the first contact with someone to when that person actually buys from me—varies from six weeks to nine months.

By printing out the entire list of people with whom I'm in conversation, and reviewing it name by name, I get a sense of the forward motion, or lack thereof in each conversation.

If I drop the ball with someone, it's not that person's responsibility to pick up the ball—it's mine, as a teacher of sales as well as a practicing salesperson. I'm a bit more in the hot seat than other sellers because I've got to practice what I preach. In fact, I've closed deals with people largely based on the fact that I stayed with them over a period of time and did not drop the ball.

> The caveat for sales professionals is not to assume that since there was forward motion in a conversation the last time you spoke to someone, that there will be forward motion at a similar pace again. Things change. Decisions are made in our absence.

Move the Sale Forward

Even though Isaac Newton felt that we would have constant forward motion, there are outside forces that influence or disturb the process. When outside forces, like priorities and emergencies, come into play, they affect the constant motion forward.

According to Newton, when outside unbalanced forces work on something, that thing doesn't stay in motion or that thing doesn't stay at rest. It'll shift direction or move or come to a complete stop.

People's priorities change. Emergencies or concerns about our offer, which did not exist during our pervious conversation, can rear their ugly heads.

If you stop calling, e-mailing or even postal mailing newsletters, articles of interest, etc., your conversations will sit at rest and probably stay there unless you do something about it. Conversely, conversations that are in motion will stay in motion as long as you pay attention, stay organized and invest some effort.

Newton's outside forces can be counterbalanced by the salesperson's persistence.

The ultimate goal of moving conversations forward is the motivation behind each contact you make. Keep your eye on the long-term relationship and apply imagination by seeing *through* the transaction, instead of *to* the transaction.

By answering the *What* questions, you'll have a greater sense of being organized. You know who you want to speak to or see on each given day and you know what you want to talk to them about, as well as what you want as a result.

A side benefit of organization is progress that can be measured. Many sales people go home every Friday night without having closed business that week. Maybe this experience is a regular part of how you make your living.

If this is the case, the only way you can go home with a sense of accomplishment is to have something else to measure—outside of the dollars or number of transactions that week.

You can count calls, conversations, meetings, proposals sent and other things to show yourself that you're generating activity in a specific and directed manner. This gives you an ability to measure your performance via multiple indices.

When? Sales people are always looking for the best time to call or contact prospects. Some will tell you that the early morning is the best time to engage in cold calling. Others will tell you to cold call at the end of the day. Still, others will tell you to make sure that you call during the traditional lunch hours, maybe between 11:30 A.M. and 1:30 P.M.

All of these are correct. We can create in our minds a multitude of reasons why something should not happen. If we call too early in the day, people have not had a chance to get their day going. If we wait too long into the day, they will be in meetings and will not want to be disturbed by a salesperson. We begin, again, to act as our own worst enemy.

The best time for someone to pick up the phone and call other people is *right now*. (As long as you know who and what you're calling about.)

Conclusion

This chapter focused on the first two of eight elements to selling professionally. *Imagination* and *organization* are two of the most important, as they will help you more effectively achieve the other elements. A few things to remember from this chapter, which will prepare you for the next one on strong openings:

➡ Using your imagination to engage customers in conversations is key to moving conversations forward and sustaining long-term sales.

➡ Imagination means seeing the conversation as a unit of process—a way of making transactions not just on a business level but on a human level.

➡ Achieving productive conversation requires:

- asking open-ended questions;

- learning about the potential buyer and his or her business; and

- celebrating the process of making these human connections rather than the ultimate sale.

➡ The 80/20 Pareto Principle applies to sales: Eighty percent of the sales are made by 20 percent of the sales people; 80 percent of our job as sellers, communicators, etc. is *listening*; and 20 percent of our job is *responding*.

➡ Having a daily plan and organizing your day will generate the best results.

➡ Being organized means answering: *Who? What?* and *When?*

You're well on your way to selling professionally. In the next chapter, we'll delve into the guts of conversations by detailing powerful openings. A strong opening is required for you to get a conversation going in the first place. Only then will you be able to move the conversation, and in turn, the sale, forward.

CHAPTER 4:
STRONG OPENINGS

Cold calling is the absolute bane of the professional salesperson—especially for someone new to sales. It's like paying taxes and meeting your future in-laws at the same time.

Does this make you want to pick up the phone and start cold calling? Probably not.

You may smirk as you read this, but my goal is not to sugar coat the concepts. It's to present the reality along with useful approaches that can actually make cold calling (and certainly the rest of the selling process) more productive, less stressful, more rewarding…and fun.

The Hard Part of Being a Sales Professional

Cold calling is difficult for three very specific reasons:

- We are not born with the ability to cold call well;

- People are more likely to reject a proposal from someone they don't know; and

- We tend to set up expectations that are not supported by actual facts.

Move the Sale Forward

Since no one is born a great cold caller, these issues apply to you. Expectation management rears its head, and will continue to, throughout your selling career. As you reach a new level of effectiveness, there will be a wellspring of confidence that comes along with the achievement.

> When someone can do something that most people cannot (and they do it reasonably well), he or she inspires confidence. My caution to you is that, as you reach each plateau of proficiency in this profession, the stakes get higher, the risks required to grow become larger and the potential for failure increases. Keep working on your strong openings with prospects—even if you know you're pretty good.

Be aware of your own progress. Look for new ways to learn more and make higher connections. The good news is that when you win, you win bigger and bigger…as long as you manage your expectations. This begins, of course, in a strong opening—the focus of this chapter.

As part of your being organized in your selling process, you must have specific goals for each contact with a prospect or client. And, before you can move conversations forward, you must begin the process with an opening. The law of inertia comes into play again here, as once you open a conversation and get it moving, you hope to keep it moving in a forward direction. Every time you start a new conversation with someone you've never met previously, you're taking a risk.

We have already stated that the first person to ask three questions in a row has taken control of the conversation. This is not to imply that control cannot be won back. Control may flow back and forth between two people—between you and your prospect.

Our first area of focus should be the great opening, which is not designed to make the other person buy. The great opening begins the conversation by stating specific information, then asking a question or two. It's something you must redesign, retool and rebuild regularly. As you work through your prospect/customer list, you'll begin to tire of saying the same thing over and over. You'll gather a handful of great openings that you'll interchange to see which ones work, when and with whom.

Cold calling is initiation. It's bold, brazen and unnerving. There is no crystal ball you can consult for knowing the potential to do business with anyone you choose to call.

The great opening works as follows:

- It answers the questions that people between you and the key decision maker (potential customer) need to know before sending you forward.

- It engages and involves that person, by asking an open-ended question, preferably one that contains an emotional trigger word.

- It sets up reasonable expectations for the current conversation.

- It helps them to dispatch you quickly; and

- It prevents them from feeling as though they are being sold something.

This is a formidable list of requirements for an interaction that can last as little as 35 seconds. There's a fine line here between confidence and cockiness. You must be in tune with their rhythm and avoid stepping on their toes.

The four components to the great opening:

➥ Identify yourself;

➥ Identify your company;

Move the Sale Forward

➡ State your reason for the call; and

➡ Ask an open-ended killer question.

The third component deserves first attention. This is where most sales people have the hardest time. One of the challenges for many seasoned sales professionals is telling someone else what it is they do, offer and sell.

When you ask sales people what they do for a living, they are sometimes hard-pressed to give you a clear, succinct statement. It's hard for sales people because they often lose sight of what's exciting about their work. They describe it in cold, unemotional terms. This is contrary to the enthusiasm they display when working on a big deal. Why the confusion? Because sales—especially in the corporate setting—is more of a process than most sales people admit even to themselves.

Ask yourself: What do you do exactly? It may take you time to answer, and when you do, note if you say one of the following:

- "I sell real estate."

- "I get people jobs."

- "I put phone systems in."

- "I'm in sales."

If you said any of the above, you probably won't capture the interest of a casual acquaintance. These are not very inviting responses. You aren't giving people a mental picture of how what you do makes a difference or can help someone else's business.

The portion of the great opening that's most difficult and requires the most creativity is explaining the reason for the call. On the surface, it doesn't seem too difficult to articulate, but it can be. A great opening is the "high concept" part of the sale. It's the most open-ended…the least specific.

Since most sales people are detail driven, they trip up here. A great opening establishes who's who and what's at stake. It sets the stage for the sale—which comes later.

The strong opening stands in the way of many sales professionals because they're programmed to feeling as though they need to fill every moment of silence with statements, sounds, questions and pitches. The result? They forget the key reasons for people buying from them.

> **Those reasons have to do with a sense of comfort, a sense of trust and the impression that the salesperson listens to them. Need cannot be the only reason, nor the key motivating reason people buy from a particular representative.**

Great openings are so tough for some sales people that they try to avoid openings altogether. How? Networking. They hope that meeting prospects in a setting that mixes business and pleasure will establish a sales context automatically. I'm all for business networking but it doesn't help much with the opening skills you need when you're making a cold call.

To my mind, the best way to build a strong opening is to spend a minute analyzing what works best in your business with existing clients.

Ask clients why they continue to do business with you year after year. Their answers will give you something to think about as you approach potential new customers and clients.

Your reasons for calling could be one of many:

- to introduce yourself;
- to find out who'd be the best point of contact for dealing with your offer;

- to determine the best way to contact that person;

- to circle back around ("We spoke a few weeks/days ago, and Joe asked me to circle back around…");

- to continue the conversation;

- to get their opinions of some introductory information they requested;

- to learn more; and

- to return their call.

When I was an executive recruiter, I learned that Human Resources wasn't the best point of contact for my pitches. It made more sense to speak directly with the person to whom my candidate would report to in the organization. Generally, people who are in a reasonably high position are the best people to begin conversations with regarding what you offer. To sell sales training, I ask for the person "most in charge of sales." Although approval may come from someone else, you want to know what's truly needed before you make any kind of offer.

When thinking about your reasons for calling a prospect or customer, stay away from a salesy mentality that tries to think of calls as steps to closing deals. You need to re-program your mind to think of calls as ways of forwarding conversations.

Sales and Quality Management

When you start thinking of sales as a process—a conversation moving forward—you can see how it fits in with other business processes. One comparison that I like is between sales and quality management.

American business has adopted the total quality management (TQM) philosophy, the idea that the best way for companies to ensure their own survival and growth is to regularly elicit feedback from their customers. According to the TQM philosophy, in order for a company to be successful, quality improvement programs must be management-led and customer-oriented, which may require fundamental changes in the way companies and agencies do business.

Companies need to know how well their products/services are living up to the expectations of customers—and this is what TQM aims to do. Many purchasing executives are convinced that a large percentage of sales people have trouble following up with an existing client because they're afraid something might have gone wrong with the product or service.

This flies in the face of TQM, which has since become a business method that U.S. companies practice diligently. Those that succeed are honored with the prestigious Malcolm Baldridge Award for Quality. This award is given out by the National Institute of Standards and Technology, a branch of government that rewards the private sector for quality management. It was established in 1988 and named after the man who served as Secretary of Commerce from 1981 until his death in 1987.

> **The existence of this movement and the awards that go with practicing TQM make one thing clear: Companies are in business to generate a profit and they will best generate profits when clients and customers become enraptured with what they offer and want to buy it again and again.**

Some people might shutter at the suggestion that quality management is a sales function. But I firmly believe that the two processes are alike...and related. TQM tells us that we need to be in touch with our customers, work on improving what they receive from us, how they receive it and how it performs after they receive it.

Move the Sale Forward

In the face of TQM, companies have to ask themselves:

- What is the value of what we offer?

- How many customers have we lost because we were not focused on quality?

- How many new customers can we win now that we are committed to quality?

- How is our offer perceived?

- Why do our current customers buy from us?

Sales people almost never ask these last two questions, yet they need to. Marketing experts and research people ask these types of questions all the time. Customers are looking for continuous improvement. Sales people are looking for continuous revenue.

These last two questions must be continually asked at the salesperson's level, because when someone decides to do business with the salesperson, he or she is looking forward to a return on investment as a natural outcome to the seller-buyer relationship.

A good way to build emotional capital with prospects is to gather as many testimonials as you can. Date them and keep diligent records. These will come in handy when a potential client asks to see one. When people read a testimonial letter, they are looking for confirmation of their decision to buy from you.

As you go forward in your sales career, you will collect more and more testimonials. When people are satisfied with the work you perform for them, they are often willing to take a moment to write their comments and mail them to you. As is consistent with human nature, they will rarely do this without being prompted.

> Ask for testimonials from your best customers. It may sound like you're asking a lot—and there's always the risk that they'll decline—but if you target your most satisfied customers, you'll most likely get some very positive comments to add to your bag of tricks.

The Power of Testimonials

Perhaps the best tool for a strong opening is a testimonial from a satisfied client. A testimonial can establish a lot in a short time—that you've delivered your product or service; that it's worked as promised; that you know your market; and that you have at least some experience. Asking for a testimonial definitely qualifies as a calculated risk because the person has already indicated his or her level of satisfaction with the work. That is why, in order to gather testimonials, follow these guidelines:

- Wait for clients to experience what you offer before you ask them what they think;

- Wait for clients to make a positive comment without you prompting them to say good things;

- Once they make the comment, do not ask a yes/no question such as: "Would you mind writing that out and sending it to me?"

- Phrase your question in an open-ended manner: "How would you feel about sending me a letter with those comments?" Or: "How would you feel about putting what you just said on letterhead and mailing that to our office?" See if they would be willing to reference you specifically in the letter.

- Make it clear that this is not a letter from the customer to your boss. This is a To Whom It May Concern letter that they (by their own choice) write and mail. You want it to be similar to Letters to The Editor in popular magazines.

Remember: Ask for the testimonial on their company letterhead. Personal notes are great, but when someone puts comments on company letterhead, he or she is willing to back it up if anyone ever researches your testimonials.

It may seem odd to think about testimonials when planning a great opening, but there is a correlation. The best way for you to help other people discover what you do and why you might be valuable to them, is to describe your offering using other people's comments. Sales people tend to get caught up in their own lingo, using obtuse language when talking to customers.

Customers speak the language of their business, not your product. That can mean a lot to someone else in their business.

What one happy customer says about your offering—the way it was delivered and the reliability of the salesperson—is worth a thousand beautifully designed brochures. Beyond showing someone the letter, it's useful to have people describe to you:

- What you do;

- Why you are unique; and

- Why they hired you in the first place.

Club Corporation of America, a company that owns and manages over 230 high-end golf courses, country clubs and private dinner clubs around the world, follows a simple and elegant rule of thumb for goal setting and managing meetings. Michele Carroll, their Senior VP of Revenue, says it's a good idea to begin a conversation with the end in mind. In other words, when you plan your opening, keep your overall goals in mind—which are never getting a sale necessarily. As mentioned many times before, your goals should include making human connections, moving conversations forward and getting the other person to feel good about the process.

The Mechanics of a Strong Opening

A great opening is not the silver bullet or the golden key that will open all doors for you. A great opening will, however, give your conversations, and the relationships resulting from them, some frame of reference. As sales professionals, you're always challenged to convey what is in your head to others in a way that will get others to respond—and move forward.

Getting the kids in bed, angling for a raise at work or doing well in an interview are nerve-racking experiences. Starting a selling conversation from scratch, via the great opening, is equally as difficult. You want people to be as excited about what you offer as you are. You want them to know that you're professional, reliable and even fun to work with. But people need to find those things out on their own. This is why the opening must be designed to be just an opening. It is not the entire conversation, much less the relationship.

Move the Sale Forward

> Don't sabotage your chance to move forward in a conversation by getting too excited about and focused on what you want to say in your opening. Keep things simple and relaxed. Don't try to get everything into your opening at the loss of your potential customer.

If you're calling to get an appointment with someone you've never met, you're probably going to run into some resistance. If you're calling to get an order with someone you haven't done business with in a long time, you may receive the rude awakening that since you have not contacted that person in months, he or she may have been buying from your competitor. These scenarios are examples of reasons why you need to make sure you arm yourself with a great opening—before you open your mouth.

First, provide the answer to three questions up front:

1) Your name;

2) Your company name; and

3) Why you are calling.

As we mentioned, the last answer is the most challenging. Your statements, while outlining every detail about your product, why others buy it and how it trounces the competition, are not issues for potential customers. On the other hand, customers want to know immediately what to do with your call. They want to identify the *purpose* of your call clearly and quickly.

Examples of what you can say:

- The reason I am calling is I wanted to introduce myself to the most appropriate person that would handle _____.

- We help companies like yours _____ and I was calling to see who the best person would be for me to speak to.

- We are in the business of_____ and I came across the name of your company in an article. It mentions Jim Johnson. How involved in _____ is Mr. Johnson?

- I'm phoning today to speak to the person you think is the most appropriate person to introduce myself to.

These examples are designed for the screener (i.e., the gatekeeper), and not necessarily the key decision maker. But keep in mind that anyone who decides whether you make it to the next step, or the next person, is a decision maker. The *key* decision maker is the one who can approve the transaction without someone else's blessing.

When you call or see a key decision maker for the first time, your opening is just as important. It must be rehearsed and ready to go so you sound relaxed and confident.

When addressing him or her, follow the rules set out above. Decision makers are in the business of evaluating sales people, their offers and ability to deliver a good offer.

A Template for a Great Opening

"Hi, My name is _____ and I am with _____ and the reason I am calling is to introduce myself, to see if what we offer might be of use or value to you. What's the best way for us to determine that?"

Move the Sale Forward

> "Hi, my name is _____ and I am with _____ and I was calling to see if you might have a minute to talk."

Sales people intrigue most folks in an opening because people want to hear "the pitch." Take any invitation to go forward by delivering a good reason for your call, and then follow it with an open-ended killer question. Make sure not to run off at the mouth. You don't want to tell the key decision maker everything up front. You may want to mention a generalized statement about what you offer, and ask the key decision maker how it might be of use or value to him or her.

> **Let's say you present the issue more as a statement than a question: "I'm calling to see if you might have a minute to talk." If their response sounds like: "Well, I have a minute..." keep a close eye on the clock during your prospect's answer and point out the time when you reach the limit he or she grants you.**

For example, say: "You said you'd give me a minute, and we are at 55 seconds." A great majority of people will encourage you to continue talking. At least you've shown respect for their time, and that you keep your word. It's about the prospect and what he or she needs—not you and your sales pitch.

Put yourself in the position of the receptionist at a busy office. She has sales people walking in the door all day. She has people looking for job applications. She has people delivering things that someone ordered, and that person is out sick today, and the delivery person insists that if delivery is not accepted, there will be an additional charge and the person who ordered it will have to pay because the receptionist did not accept delivery, and…then someone like you calls.

You want to be friendly with the person; you want to know how the weather is on her side of town. You ask questions as inane as "How are you doing today?" She is expected to keep her cool, be calm, friendly and answer every question you ask without sounding impatient. You start to sell your product over the phone, to someone without the authority to buy. You start asking detailed questions about things like when her company's lease on the office ends, to whether or not her employer uses a payroll service or if there are any people in the office that might be interested in a lower priced cell phone plan.

That receptionist who answered your call isn't interested in the long answer. That receptionist wants to get to the heart of the matter and get on with her life. Your desire to determine whether or not this company is going to be a waste of time doesn't enter the receptionist's mind.

So, rewind to the great opening. There are *four components to a strong identification statement*:

➡ Identify yourself;

➡ Identify your company;

➡ State your purpose for the call; and

➡ Ask an open-ended killer question.

You are bound to confront obstacles like moody gatekeepers in your pursuit of selling. Knowing you'll face a certain obstacle helps you prepare for the obstacle. Nothing will guarantee that you'll overcome every obstacle, but preparation will help you better manage those obstacles—and the potential for rejection.

Move the Sale Forward

The gatekeepers, or the *screeners*, are always a problem for sales people. And many sales professionals are not too skilled in dealing with these people and the problems they bring to the conversation. Sellers are often quick to judge a screener as someone who hates all sales people. Screeners generally don't care about your great openings. They want to get to the heart of the conversation and don't really want an invitation to move forward. Allow them to dispatch your call. The sooner you give them a reason to pass you through, the better.

You might cover a niche market and be the only one selling your brand in that market, but chances are you are competing with someone. This is why the opening is so much more important than the closing. When you try to close someone, you're working to influence that person. You're trying to make a living, which is honorable, but the intent—the motivation—is just as important to you as an advocate for forward motion sales as are the actual results.

You want to increase your ability to connect with people. That can only result in your finding out more about people's businesses and their way of thinking. Hopefully, that will lead to opportunities to present solutions…and earn a living. Your self-confidence and self-esteem will increase if your product or service brings direct, lasting value to the people who use it.

The more openings you create, the more people you have the potential to connect with. This eventually means more business for you.

 Remember: The more openings you create, the more people you connect with…and the greater your potential to move conversations forward and create sales.

As the ideas we discuss here develop into a workable plan, the way you sell and communicate will change. You won't be changing your personality, but you'll learn better ways of responding to people and taking conversations forward.

Conclusion

People are reasonably savvy. As soon as you start to sell, people can tell. Focus on the human connection in every sale, transaction and relationship you establish...and start with a good opening. You'll earn money as a result of offering and delivering something of value to people, as a result of meaningful conversations. Instead of thinking about pitches, think about conversations, opportunities to learn more about people, what they like and dislike...and how you can help them achieve their goals.

Among the most important tools you'll use in conjunction with your strong openings is what I call the 20 Call Burst. It's such a vital component to your selling that I've dedicated the next chapter to the topic. You can't pick up the phone and use your strong openings unless you know who you're going to call and what you're overall goals are for every call you make. This is where the 20 Call Burst comes into play, and Chapter 5 will define and describe exactly what this means.

Move the Sale Forward

CHAPTER 5:

THE 20 CALL BURST

I started my career in sales by working in an employment agency in New York City. I had just completed four years in the Navy, and moved back to the New York area. A good friend was working at the agency, and he encouraged me to come in and see if they could place me in a job. I was sent out on interviews; one was for an assistant manager's position in a retail store. Another was as a mailroom clerk. Neither of these was particularly exciting, so I went back to sit in the agency until someone sent me on another interview. The was the beginning of my sales career.

Interviewee to Interviewer

After 10 days of watching what the counselors did, I began to ask questions. Why do they jump up and ring a bell, two or three times a day? What do the numbers they keep hanging on the board above their desks mean? What's a sales commission? And then finally: How can I get a job doing what you people do?

I got a straightforward answer: People jump up and ring the bell when they make a placement (i.e., they close a sale).

If a candidate from the agency had been hired, that meant a fee would be paid to the agency. As a result, a commission would be paid to the counselor. This was cause for celebration, hence the clanging of the bell.

Move the Sale Forward

I thought, this is easy enough! Sit at a nice desk, in a decent office, right near the financial district in the Big Apple…and get paid commission.

Where do I sign up?

The manager sat me down and asked if I thought I could starve for six months. In a commission/draw environment, you can work for a significant period of time before you "get off draw," or collect commissions that exceed the draw you bring home. Commissions replace the draw as your income. Since you receive draw (i.e., a loan) from the first week of work, it can take some time to see real money. In typical New York fashion, I pointed out: "I'm not making any money sitting here every day."

"Okay," she said, "here's the deal. You start at $100 per week, draw. You are required to obtain two spots (i.e., open positions at companies) per week." Once I acquired two spots I was allowed to market them to the other counselors. The scene was absolute chaos. Forty loud-mouthed New Yorkers would market their spots, their candidates (also known as "apps"—for applicant) across the desk or across the room. It was so much fun, it's hard to imagine that I ever left. It was like the trading floor of the stock exchange—but we were putting employees and employers together, instead of stocks and investors.

I couldn't wait to get home to my wife (of 30 days) and tell her the amazing news. I thought she'd be thrilled to learn how much money I could potentially make. She'd understand why we'd gotten married and moved from California to New York. I was now a personnel placement counselor…and I'd even get business cards.

My first day was great—meeting everyone again, not as someone looking for a job, but as a counselor. One of *them*.

Then, I was shown to my desk. It had two phones on it. "One for outgoing, one for incoming," I was told. "The only one you will need right now is the outgoing."

I was handed a copy of the Manhattan Yellow Pages.

"Okay," the manager said. "Get to work!"

I was not sure what specifically I was supposed to do, which must have shone on my face.

"You need to get some spots, so you can make some placements," she said.

I blinked.

"John. Here's the Manhattan phone book. All the companies are in here. Get on the phone, find some spots and quote them our fee. If they agree to see your people, then you have an agreement. Don't come to me with any spots where you haven't quoted the fee. If you do, and anyone in the office sends their people out, they get hired, and the counselor doesn't get their fee, they won't work with you anymore. Ever. Clear?"

"Crystal," I replied. Obviously, I was expected to bring something to the party in addition to my optimism and energy.

She turned on her heel and walked back to her desk. In the first hour, I remember four people coming up to my desk and asking: "Got any spots?"

It was clear to me that it was time to get into the game. I started looking through the phone book and listening to the people at desks near mine. I heard some things that sounded like good ways to get people to give me spots, but I failed horribly throughout the day and went home dejected.

I realized the second day that I'd received all the training they'd give me. This was a sink or swim environment and all the counselors had found a way to swim...or were on their way out. I received a yellow tablet for taking notes. When I asked for a pen, I was told that the stationery store was down the street. This was where I discovered that it was up to me to produce something. No one was going to do it for me.

Frustration soon set in. If selling was so important to business, why didn't anyone teach the basics? Why was it so much about trial and error? Successful athletes have coaches; successful doctors and lawyers have teachers; so why doesn't selling have at least some form of instruction?

Move the Sale Forward

This is when I took a hard look at whether or not I had made the right decision. I asked colleagues how long they thought it took to actually get going in this business.

I looked for guidance from those who looked competent, professional, and most of all, made money consistently. What did they think it took to achieve what they had? Why did so many people who had apparent potential fail? What was the dividing line? Are there truly secrets?

My fellow comrades' answers are still with me:

- Stay focused, and don't spend more time socializing in the office than cold calling new clients;

- Ask for referrals;

- Listen to what people say in the interview with you—they may blow an interview with a client because you don't prepare them properly;

- Make sure the dollars associated with the deal are clear and openly discussed *prior* to engaging in the relationship;

- Admit when you screwed up;

- Try to listen more than you talk; and

- See if what you're doing actually helps all involved.

Lacking a dedicated, structured training plan in this company, and not wanting to get to know brand new employees every few days, I took it upon myself to help people new to the sales job whenever I could. I noticed that smart, hardworking people were coming in and out of the sales profession like riders on the subway. On at one stop, off at the next.

Those who'd found a way to swim were finding ways to survive—and were enjoying it. Whenever people were put at a desk near me, I'd ask them questions about what brought them to the company and what they hoped to get out of working there. I'd inquire about their background and the things they liked to do on the weekends. This is when I first realized the power of listening.

☞ **Point of Impact #5:** The more you listen to what others have to say, the more fascinating they'll find you.

I also learned that directed activity is more effective than charm or personal contacts. It took a few years to learn how to manage the amount of outbound calls I would make in order to get a foothold in a vertical market. Once I found my own way to swim, I enjoyed some success with the employment agency.

I had earned the coveted Counselor of the Month award and felt I had accomplished something of note. I got beyond living on draw and started to see real income.

But looking back, the most valuable thing I got out of that work experience was a firsthand look at how people sabotage their own success. I saw firsthand how vulnerable we are when we seek employment.

> When you have to look for work, you often enter the interview at a disadvantage. You feel that what you have to offer has value, but that the person interviewing you gets to decide whether or not to hire you. If you don't get hired, you feel wounded and unworthy, which worsens your negotiating ability.

Until we have a place to go, a function to perform and a paycheck to anticipate, we devalue ourselves as people. Most of us derive a percentage of our value as a person from the work that we do. How prestigious it is, how well it pays, what sort of room for advancement there might be, etc.

Sales people are guilty of using their client list as an indicator of how well-positioned they are. It helps us feel unique and able to bring something good to the table. When we go out looking for work, we often make the mistake of believing we're not good enough. We make excuses for our shortcomings.

Making these discoveries helped me shift my perspective toward what selling was all about. Instead of only interviewing people because I felt they would generate a fee for me quickly, I learned how to connect with and respond to this vulnerability, which allowed me to be more in tune with them as people.

The interview process causes fear and distress in many. It's one of the purest forms of selling in the world.

Interviewing as a Sales Technique

What we do helps define who we are. Without any tangible proof (outside of the application we fill out or the résumé we produce) that we can perform a function, or provide a service, we must sell ourselves to the potential employer. This is selling an intangible to a presumably skeptical buyer in a short amount of time. Navigating an interview in such a way where the interviewer does as much talking as the interviewee (or even more) is the ideal situation.

Interviewing is the purest form of selling because we are selling something that does not exist: potential. Over the years, while coaching friends, former clients and friends of friends through the work search maze, the ability to define one's service has been the biggest challenge for people. My challenge to people looking for work is to clearly and briefly define their service in terms that will show some sort of value to the potential employer (customer). Once that service is defined in clear, simple language, it's time to start getting out there and determining who to offer it to.

By thinking about how to help the folks I couldn't place (due to their lack of experience, for example), I discovered how to better market myself, my spots and other applicants. Once their service was clearly defined, I could then find the most likely person or company who would find that service valuable. This was a turning point in my approach to sales. I realized that there were no different rules or requirements to selling the service of the employment agency than were applicable to selling apps in the office to other counselors. Selling was no longer the focus of what I did and how I approached people—it was the natural result of what I did and how I approached people.

> **Whatever you're selling, you must systematically and logically call on your target market. If it takes you an average of 3.5 dials to get a decision maker on the phone you must divide your tasks and time. You must look at the calendar and plot out what you want to have happen and when.**

In order to gain control of your desk and business you must employ the third step for selling professionally: Discipline. Discipline comes from a root word, which is "disciple." A disciple is traditionally viewed as a follower, someone who follows a regular, proven path. Thus, in order to manage, understand and master your process, you must exercise discipline.

Remember: Sales typically has some high moments as well as some very low moments. If you discipline yourself toward the task, you'll best be able to focus, bring emotion into the equation and measure your progress. If you can measure what you do, you can track results. This, in turn, will allow you to improve upon your past performance.

The 20 Call Burst

One of the most powerful tools a salesperson can have is the ability to make 20 consecutive calls to potentially new customers as well as old contacts. A 20 Call Burst is a specific, directed activity that immediately gives you control over your selling day. There's no right time to make these calls; so long as you have a dial tone you can make calls.

> The best time to make outbound calls, including cold calls, is...right now.

The first 20 Call Burst of the day should be done soon after you arrive at the office. It should not be relegated to a specific time of the day, nor should you limit yourself to one 20 Call Burst per day. A simple rule of thumb is: If you have more time than you have business, then do another 20 Call Burst. We look for a reason why certain people may not be receptive or we think about how effective we might be at one point of the day as opposed to another. All of these are excuses. It's simple: Plan a 20 Call Burst as soon as possible. Make the calls as soon as possible. Plan the next one as soon as possible. Make the next 20 Call Burst ASAP.

Companies selling anything from vitamins to enterprise software have adopted this approach. From commercial real estate to employment services. From industrial metal to consulting services. From headsets to video conferencing. From Internet services to cellular phones. From high-end hospitality to employment and staffing services. If you maintain any part of your business relationships over the phone (which you probably do), then the 20 Call Burst is a necessary tool for you. It'll increase your sense of control over your business and future. Combining it with intuitive contact management software will give you an advantage over your competition.

And the beauty of it is simplicity.

When sales people sit down to generate outbound calls, they are surrounded and bombarded by distractions. Among the most distracting is an interested buyer. Assume, for example, Suzy Salesperson is sitting at her desk at 9:35 A.M. On her desk are a variety of things: a pricelist, a catalogue, a computer, some business cards of prospects, a personal calendar, pictures of friends and family, a coffee cup, pens, paper clips, birthday cards, new faxes, old faxes, printed e-mails, new memos, product updates and competitive information.

You know what to expect. She begins her day—starting with a phone call. She dials, gets voice mail and hangs up. She looks through some articles that her boss gave her, then picks up a note about a potential new customer. She mentally debates calling, then dials. The receptionist is less than cooperative; Suzy gets a bit flustered. She bows out of the call, then returns to the matters most pressing on her desk. Something was supposed to ship yesterday—did it? Is it still in the building? Better check.

Her phone rings. It's a client. They don't want to buy anything; they just wanted to ask a question. While she's on the phone, someone comes to her desk and asks about lunch. It's 9:40 A.M. Once she indicates that she'll call the co-worker upon completion of this call, the co-worker departs and Suzy's other line rings. Not wanting to be rude to the current customer on the line, she lets the call go to voice mail.

Finally, the customer is satisfied. Suzy gets off the phone and checks voice mail.

It turns out to be a call sent to her desk by mistake, but she knows whose customer it is, so she walks around the office trying to find the person who works on that account.

It's 10:15 A.M. now, almost 45 minutes after her initial outbound dial. She feels it's time for a well-deserved break.

How many outbound calls did Suzy make? Two.

It's easy to allow the outside world to eat up your time. You may have seen a commercial that ran a lot on T.V. It depicted a typical office: The first cubicle is packed with people celebrating a birthday; the second has someone using his computer to download music; the third is a woman on speakerphone with a friend.

The commercial ends with an announcer saying: "Another great reason not to work in the office." The company that put out the ad was in the business of selling cellular phones. And their point was well taken.

> **Your job as a salesperson is to create—and move forward—as many conversations as you can with qualified buyers. The best way for you to take control of your desk and day is to generate 20 Call Bursts.**

Regardless of the size of your database, snatch up 20 business cards. Make sure these are 20 people who meet your specific qualifying criteria. If this takes a long time, you've been experiencing less than stellar results with your selling efforts, and that's okay. You're learning. Once you have

20 leads, clear everything off your desk and make some quick notes about these people:

- Where did you get the card?

- What do these people do in their respective positions?

- What do you know about the company?

- How long has it been since you called, wrote, e-mailed, or met them?

- What possible reason would they have to want to speak with you?

Assume they don't know anything about you and your company or product. In addition, even though you have a great memory for faces and events, they may not. Also realize that your decision to call doesn't mean that they've been waiting by the phone, eager and ready to speak with you.

With these 20 leads, let's go through an exercise that will incorporate many of the ideas we've already discussed. Start dialing with one goal: finding someone with whom you can move the conversation forward. Once you begin, don't be distracted by voice mail, screeners, busy decision makers, wrong extension numbers or anything else. This doesn't mean you should avoid opportunities to get appointments or disqualify customers. If you manage your expectations well, you'll have more stamina as a salesperson. You'll cover more ground in less time. You'll appear free of the need to close a deal.

> There's nothing less attractive to a potential buyer than a salesperson who appears desperate to close the deal.

Move the Sale Forward

One thing you need to accomplish in your calls: a flow. This will only happen when you avoid all distractions, as previously mentioned. Sales people are most effective when you've experienced something positive and you have no fear. This can be when you've landed an appointment with someone you've been hunting down for a long time or you're coming close to landing a two-year contract with a client. You feel as though you can slay any dragon.

This, however, isn't going to lead to better results. What happens instead is you lose your discipline to stay focused and you expend precious energy. How does this happen? After something good happens, you want to share it. You walk around the office talking with everyone and telling them about your recent accomplishment.

> **Imagine channelling all that positive energy into another outgoing call. You'd sound confident. You'd hear that confidence in your own voice. You'd look forward to the next challenge and do the smartest thing with that energy—pick up the phone and dial again.**

Once you make 20 Call Bursts a priority—and stick to them with a flow—you'll notice a difference in your results. Mix things up. Keep yourself interested. Don't do 20 cold calls in a row, if you can help it. Pepper your bursts with cold calls as well as follow-up calls. This will take some of the pressure off. If you're new to sales and must resort to 20 cold Call Bursts, don't worry: within a week you'll have a database that'll allow you to place second and third calls to prospects.

Remember: Twenty Call Bursts are exercises designed to generate a measurable number of outbound calls, the results of which will determine who goes into the next 20 Call Burst—who gets called in a week, a month and so on.

A 20 Call Burst should take about 30 to 40 minutes to prepare and 45 to 90 minutes to complete. Total time: two hours. Some sales people (including me) find a way to complete *two* rounds of 20 Call Bursts—a total of 40 calls before lunch. Make a goal to generate at least one set of 20 Call Bursts. After completing these, don't feel as though you've had a big day; the selling day is much longer than the two hours or so it takes to complete one set.

So long as you've established a database for making calls, you'll be calling new, current and old contacts (prospects, customers, etc.) so you'll have multi-layered conversations. The following is a pictoral representation of these layered conversations:

First Contact (FC) $

```
FC————————————————————>                      $
FC——————————————————————————————————>$
FC——————————————————>                         $
FC————————>                                    $
FC——————————————————————————>                 $
```

Each of the above lines is a conversation you've set in motion and are moving forward. Some of the people you call will be new, others will be on their way to doing business with you, and still some may have already done business with you and have made you money. Each conversation (not individual contact, but the larger relationship) has its own dynamics, life span and rate of progression.

When you generate a 20 Call Burst, the idea is to find out what the next step in each conversation will be. You don't want to be the one to tell the client/prospect what that step should be; rather, you want the person you are calling to tell you.

If you ask your customer where he would like to go and he gives you a destination, that's good news. If he tells you to come back next week on a particular day, you've begun a conversation.

GBH Distributing

Glendale, California-based GBH Distributing operates nine offices in seven states, and is in the business of distributing remote communication technology. Their product line ranges from telephone headsets to audio conferencing tools and video conference equipment. The company boasts over $40 million in annual sales and was founded by the current president, Von Bedikian. Bedikian's team adopted the 20 Call Burst, among other techniques, and watched his team reach a new level of success. According to Bedikian:

> The concept of moving the sale forward was something we brought into our company over three years ago. It sticks with me and I use it. The 20 Call Burst also has been a key concept in our business. We require our people to complete a minimum of one 20 Call Burst session every business day, and some can complete two. It has had a great impact; it's increased people's focus and their output, and it gets people to focus on one activity—outbound calls.

Bedikian's team was able to process information better and schedule time for the 20 Call Burst in a way that didn't interrupt the day. Bedikian notes, "My team communicates more effectively to our customers now. They are not distracted, they know what their objective is, and it becomes a process. The bottom line is making selling a process."

Sales can be a sink or swim profession. If you can't make successive calls it'll be hard to make a decent living in sales. Some of Bedikian's people didn't develop the 20 Call Burst skill...and didn't last very long at the company. The results were so great from those who started the practice that it wasn't profitable for the company to keep those who failed to make it a daily activity. He adds:

> People judge your company by who you don't fire. A 20 Call Burst is not the divining rod between who to keep and who to let go, but it really becomes evident very quickly who is passionate, and who isn't. In other words, the ones who aim to reach their selling goals look for techniques proven to work. And they usually don't have a problem using those techniques.

Not an Impossibility

Some argue that it's impossible to make 20 calls in one day. Not true. It takes discipline and stamina. I make 20 Call Bursts every day—even on the days I travel across the country. On days when I'm in the office all day, I average two sets of 20 Call Bursts. Being on the West Coast helps. I am on the phone at 7:00 A.M., calling clients in eastern time zones. Once I complete my first 20 calls, I handle e-mail, faxes and mailings, and figure out who the candidates are for my next round. I aim to get about 70 percent of my outbound calls done by noon.

Move the Sale Forward

> Caution: Two of the main distractions that sales people allow into their day are 1) answering incoming calls during their outbound efforts; and 2) acting too quickly when someone asks you to send more information.

When generating outbound efforts, you might uncover someone who's a little interested and asks you to fax, mail or e-mail information. This doesn't mean you have to jump to get that stuff out. Just because someone asks for more information doesn't mean he is ready to buy. As previously mentioned, one challenge of making the 20 Call Burst is to make it a routine whereby you don't get distracted. To see real results, you cannot let the little things interrupt you and pull you away from finishing those calls.

Think about how much more you can accomplish if you aim to make *two* 20 Call Bursts a day. If you only make one set of 20, think about your competitors who get in front of you and move conversations farther forward. Don't sell in reactive mode; be proactive by generating those calls and seeing how far you can go. How difficult would it be to get 20 leads together to call on tomorrow morning, just to see how far you get?

Conduct an experiment over the next 30 business days. Plan to make 20 Call Bursts daily. Do two sets a day if you can. Chances are you'll miss a few days but you'll probably net about 18 to 23 days of serious calling. Carve the time out in advance, do your homework with leads and prospects and get through 20 straight, uninterrupted dials.

> Never make excuses for calls on your list. Don't find ways of ducking out of calling some or all of the people you've selected to be contacted. This is called "cherry picking" or "paralysis by analysis." If you talk yourself out of calling person X, then replace that person with Y. At the very least, make 20 legitimate calls your daily goal.

Remember: nothing happens until someone sells something. And no other jobs exist until, and unless, something is being sold.

The 5 Call Objectives

Every phone call must be conducted in such a way that you accomplish the specific things you want out of the call. Of course, you want to move every conversation forward and manage your expectations well. You can do this by using the *5 call objectives*. They are to:

- Sell;
- Gather information;
- Share information;
- Establish relationships; and
- Maintain relationships.

Sell. To refresh: The definition of selling is *to have people feel good about making a positive decision and to move the conversation forward with you today*.

Notice that "close," "get the order" or "finalize the deal" are not included in the definition. Selling is not closing. Selling is not telling, either. Selling is not getting someone to do something. Selling is where you have the opportunity to make a human connection. It's where you work the hardest at focusing on the customer and treating customers like they are important people.

Move the Sale Forward

Gather information. Information is power. It is most powerful when you use it to serve customers instead of finding flaws in their thought processes. When you gather information, you're upholding the 80/20 principle by listening. Once you've listened and allowed them to talk, you can employ the third objective. When engaged in conversation, it's imperative to remember that the last eight words anyone says carry the emotional impact of the message. To this end, pay attention to these last eight words your prospect/customer says. This gives you information you can respond to.

Sharing information. You may now offer information they want to hear. Keep your comments brief and follow up any statement with a question.

Establish a relationship. Have a frame of mind whereby you aim to establish a relationship every time you pick up the phone. Be open, comfortable and prepared to make cold calls despite the number of established contacts you have.

Maintain a relationship. If you have three national accounts, you wonder when you'll get the fourth. This is when the fifth objective—maintaining relationships—comes into play. The objective helps you keep the perspective that you are not the only person who is vying for a business relationship with a given customer. You must acknowledge that your prospects and customers have lives outside of buying from you, and they have a boss, peers and colleagues who occupy their time and mind. On each call, ensure that you're living up to (or exceeding) the expectations of the buyer, and that you are appreciated. You don't want to be an inconvenience or an interruption in their day.

Maintaining a relationship means being sensitive to whether that relationship is stagnant or moving forward. Putting these objectives together, we have an equation: SELL = Gather + Share + Establish + Maintain.

When you gather and share information according to the 80/20 principle, and are regularly establishing new relationships, while maintaining existing ones with this as your approach, you cannot help but end up with selling as a result.

Conclusion

When I ask people when they think we should talk again, more conversation is what I'm looking for—not the deal. Great openings define your products and services clearly, and will get you to the next step in the selling process.

In the next chapter, we'll talk about the mechanics of moving conversations forward once you've begun them. This will include catching up with people you've talked to in the past, but have yet to close a deal with. In all, you'll learn that enthusiasm plays a big role in keeping those conversations moving in the right direction.

Move the Sale Forward

CHAPTER 6:
MOVING SALES
CONVERSATIONS FORWARD

A strong opening—as I've described—sets the process in motion. The next issues you face are:

- What do you say the next time you talk?

- If you have a conversation that's already moving, how do you get it closer to a resolution (i.e., a sale or a disqualification)?

- Does it make sense to move a particular conversation forward?

Knowing what to say the next time you talk to a prospect or customer is always tricky. But there are some guidelines, and they start with the three steps to moving conversations forward:

1) Review the past;

2) Discuss the present; and

3) Plan the future together.

Review the Past

If you're calling someone you've already spoken with at least once before, then you have a small window of opportunity to grab that person's attention, get him involved, make him comfortable and put him in a position to choose the next step.

Sounds like a tall order—and it is. This is not something that occurs because you want it to. It occurs because you've planned ahead and put a lot of thought into that planning.

People who receive a call from a salesperson want to know the point as soon as possible. So, as a salesperson, it's your job to show respect for their time and get to the point. There are certain ways to do that. For example, you could say: "Hello, Tony, it's John Klymshyn calling. The last time we spoke, you said_____."

Fill in the blank with something your prospect or customer said in the past. It's important that you not get distracted by attempting to evaluate what your prospect or customer said. Rather, the point is to show that you can repeat back to him something mentioned previously.

Put yourself in the prospect's position and think about how you'd feel if someone were able to repeat back something you said in the past. You'd feel listened to and important. If you record what someone says and call upon it in a later conversation, you'll make a good impression. You'll take that conversation to a new level.

Forty-eight percent of sales people will call a prospect once and never again. Twelve percent of sales people will call a prospect twice and never again. These are terrible statistics.

Chapter 6: Moving Sales Conversations Forward

These statistics point to the fact that some of us make attempts, and then evaluate the validity of a lead based on how difficult that person is to reach. Making two calls is not exactly a monumental effort; sales people stop far too short of the mark by abandoning the effort too early. How can you possibly evaluate, learn about and get to know someone if you don't call enough times to actually speak to the person?

Once you have endured the required persistence and get your prospect on the phone, you have 15 seconds or less to present yourself. Keep in mind what your calling party is thinking when he/she picks up the phone:

- Who's calling me?;

- What company are they with?;

- What do they want?;

- Do I want something from them?; and

- Have we spoken before, and if so, what about?

The answers to these questions are not programmed into anyone's mind, and they may not flow out of your mouth easily.

Think about your desk right now. Take a mental inventory of items on it, around it, how it is decorated and what junk there might be within arm's reach. Now imagine yourself at that desk in the middle of a fun selling day. You have a phone appointment with a prospect in about 10 minutes. You notice that your coffee cup is almost empty. Three e-mails just popped up on your screen as new deliveries and two people are having a loud conversation within five feet of you. Then your phone rings. It's someone whom you met months ago, and he is asking questions about the weather or if you watched the game last night. Sound familiar? This could easily describe your prospect's day as well.

Move the Sale Forward

I advise caution in concluding that we are "interrupting" their day. We are a regular part of their day, and our job is to make sure that we respect their time and their sense of urgency in moving things forward.

 Remember: Every decision maker on the planet wakes up every Monday morning looking for a good idea. If you have one, and are patient enough to walk your prospect through the discovery process, you will win. Regularly.

Discuss the Present

A good way to ask someone about the present is to follow up the "When we last spoke, you mentioned _____," with "What's the latest with that project?" or "What's happening there now?" Another one of my favorites: "Where are you in the process?"

When you ask: "Where are you in the process?" the person you are asking decides what process you are referring to. He/she also decides how your conversation relates to that process (if at all), and then gives you the information. You might get a response like: "There's nothing new" or "I don't have any answers yet." If you get a defensive response, back off. If you step away from the selling image, you won't ruin your reputation.

Respond instead with: "Our goal is *not* to see how quickly we can do something. Our goal is to see *if* doing something makes sense." This is a powerful response. It takes the pressure off the prospect or customer, which can open the door for letting you take the conversation farther.

When people are convinced they are the center of the universe, and you have humility, patience and confidence to treat them that way, they like it. And they will respond to you.

The Driver and the Navigator

Imagine this: You go into a store to buy something and you deal with a sales associate. If you were to step back and imagine the conversation between you and the seller being transformed into riding in a car, which seat would you like to be in?

Most people would say the driver's seat. If you were the seller (instead of the buyer), which seat would you pick? Probably the driver's seat. The problem with this is that there's only room for one person in the driver's seat and we as sales people constantly are trying to elbow the decision maker out of where the customer should be (and wants to be). Everyone wants to be in the driver's seat. Instead of wrestling for that position, put the decision makers—the buyers—in the driver's seat.

Assume you're in the passenger's seat, navigating. You're the salesperson. You're a part of the driving process and can set yourself apart from others who, instead of navigating, wrestle with the person for control. The journey is a metaphor for the conversation or larger relationship. If you can set yourself apart from others offering anything similar, or, if you can set yourself apart from anyone else out there, who is selling anything, you have achieved a rare feat.

Since they are in a position to decide whether or not you get their business, the only place that makes sense for them to be is in the driver's seat. The fact that they have the money ultimately puts them in control. Your job as a professional seller is not to dominate conversations, but to navigate them.

Plan the Future Together

Planning the future together is the final step. You want to do this while driving down the same path as your prospect or customer. You'll want to make sure you're elbow to elbow with that person, willing to let him/her drive the conversation. The 80/20 principle (80 percent listening, 20 percent responding) is especially applicable when you're moving conversations forward. It requires you to listen. Don't forget about our last Point of Impact: The more you listen to what someone has to say, the more fascinating that person finds you.

> **Review the past** ("We spoke about ___ days/weeks ago and that time you said/mentioned/asked_____); and discuss the present ("So, what's the latest?" "Where are you/we in the process?")

When you learn a new skill, you want to find ways of using it. Once you understand the mechanics behind moving the conversation forward, you can apply it to existing relationships before trying it on new business prospects. For example, imagine having someone who meets one or more of your specific qualifying criteria. It seems like she is a good prospect, but she hasn't committed to you yet. Although you've documented the conversations you've had with this person, you haven't gotten a "yes." This "yes" should be some sort of action step or statement offered or suggested by the prospect. If you actually get the word "yes," you must have asked a yes/no question—and you want to avoid this.

Your prospects become clients when *they* ask *you* questions like: "How does that date work for you?" or "Do you have a contract you can send for us to get this going?" Refrain from asking questions like: "Do you want to put that on the calendar?" or "Can we consider this a commitment?" When you indicate a requested date as being free (or confirm available inventory) your response should be something like: "I'm happy to pencil that in!" More often than not, you'll get a: "Oh, let's make sure you ink it—get your contract over to us." That's a commitment!

This is what *moving the conversation forward* is all about. In preparation for your calls, check your most recent notes. Filter out opinions and mood indicators when you take notes about conversations with prospects. Stop writing or typing useless statements like: "Doubt they will buy" or "Total Jerk." Instead, evaluate how you think you can move that conversation farther. Take their last comment, and create a statement that will combine a great opening and the three steps to move conversations forward.

> "Hello, Steve, this is _____ from _____ company. Last time we spoke, you had mentioned that some other things needed to happen prior to our conversation going forward. Where are you in that process?"

Get their attention. Put them in control. Ask them an open-ended killer question and then wait for the answer.

You need to develop a gut feeling about the truth in the answers your prospects give you. They don't lie so don't treat them as though they do. They just may not feel comfortable telling you that they won't buy from you. They have their own concerns, objectives and frustrations. You are probably not their top priority.

When your gut tells you that you have asked patient, open-ended killer questions (based on what they just said rather than what you want), that you have worked in a professional manner to move the conversation forward (not pushed, dragged or forced it), then you need to decide how much time is too much time to spend with this person.

You have a greater chance of developing a reliable gut if you do not attempt to do so in a vacuum. Talk to the senior people in your office. Ask if you can run something by them, tell them what you're planning on doing in response to what you've learned, and listen to what they say.

Make sure you don't ask for this help while your cohort is in the middle of a negotiation, or cold calling on his or her own prospect list.

 Remember: Selling can be a lonely profession at times. When things aren't going well, and you don't have that "invincible" feeling, it can be hard to get going. Picking up the phone to make a call can be overwhelming. Driving around looking for a building or a new business to cold call can be close to depressing. But this is one of the many rites of passage required for success. It's the gate through which you must find your way, prior to enjoying the business.

Getting that Enthusiasm

When a deal slips through your fingers, it's difficult to get back on the horse for another ride. Some of us have to commiserate. We have to sit and think about why we didn't get the sale. We might walk around the office and tell everyone how close we came. As emotional people, we often look for solace or a pity partner.

The best way to generate enthusiasm, regardless of your mood, level of confidence or desire to commiserate, is to find a time to get together with people who do the same work as you. It's wasteful to take time in the middle of the day to complain about lost deals. Instead, set aside time to share your experiences with other sellers—but do this outside the selling day.

> When you share stories with other sellers during prime selling hours, be prepared to hear others' disappointments. You don't want them to impact your enthusiasm during your day.

Enthusiasm is supposed to come from within, but that means having a less than realistic attitude. You can't show up to work thinking that every deal is going to close. You're also expected to have an attitude that makes others want to be around you. No one wants a salesperson to sound unenthusiastic.

The best way to generate enthusiasm is to be around people who face the same challenges you do. This means being with people who share the same goals and dreams as you do. When you set aside time with other sellers, pick the people who understand your vision, your dreams and can offer useful words of encouragement or an understanding ear.

Let's be clear. We are not robotic, stoic, uncaring people. Most sellers have a passion. A passion for life, for challenges and for their chosen profession. My encouragement is that you try to manage your emotions and be aware of how freely you share what's affecting you within the confines of the office.

An informal discussion in a neutral environment (walking through the local mall, sitting in a hotel lobby or even on the way to your car) are perfect places to let off steam or explore the possible reasons a deal did not come through. The selling floor—or doorway to someone else's office—is not.

Move the Sale Forward

> Enthusiasm is powerful. It can make a world of difference in how you are perceived. It can motivate and help you to be creative when you need to be. It can make the difference in how you perform. And it doesn't come at the flip of a switch, or because you just happen to have that type of personality. It takes work and daily self-examinations.

Without enthusiasm, you could have the greatest product or service on earth and no one would want to buy it from you. Your enthusiasm is one of the intangible qualities that makes a difference in who you'll connect with, and who you won't. Enthusiasm is contagious and people want to get it from you. Once you agree that enthusiasm is an essential selling tool, you can ask yourself: "Where does it come from?"

Besides coming from within, enthusiasm requires a conscious effort. You can't mentally check out at 10 A.M. just because you win—or lose—a deal.

Think about a time you've gotten together with fellow entrepreneurs or sales people to tell each other how you'd run one another's businesses. It's a great forum for idea sharing, boasting and stealing great ideas from folks who are happy to provide something useful. To that end, enthusiasm also comes from *sharing experiences* and *sharing ideas*. You can probably recall dozens of times you've shared ideas with people, which sparked greater ideas and debate, and all of you accomplished more.

> Enthusiasm is the spark that gets things done. When enthusiasm bounces between two people, or three or among 30, they all start to feel more alive. It's a natural high.

When you share your experiences and make human connections, you almost react the way atoms do when they're in close proximity. They begin to shake, vibrate and generate heat. In all, they get things moving!

Without enthusiasm, you cannot be excited about what you have to offer, nor can you make customers enthusiastic about buying from you. There's a very old book in which it says: "An iron sharpens iron, so one person sharpens another."

Club Corporation's Experience

We introduced ClubCorp, Inc., the world's largest owner and operator of private country clubs, business clubs and sports club, in Chapter 4. The company began to implement the concepts outlined in this book back in 1994. The company operates with a sales force of over 200 people.

My first session with ClubCorp focused on the 20 Call Burst. At that time, Michele Carroll, Senior VP of Revenues for the company and was the regional sales manager for Southern California. He was responsible for 24 clubs. According to Carroll:

> I first brought [this] approach inside the company because of the focus on discipline for sales people. Our relationship evolved into dealing with the entire process. A disciplined process is what I personally liked. At the time, we were selling according to *features*, *features* and *features*. Particularly in the private club business, we were more interested in our folks developing relationships, as opposed to simple open probe, closing question approaches that are out there. We wanted to get a shift going on towards the relationship, as opposed to the feature, or hard-core widget sale.

During my work with ClubCorp., it was common for me to hear things like: "I never thought about that aspect before." Of course, the sales people were referring to my human connection approach. As Carroll points out:

> "Yes, my folks knew it was important to be friendly, kind, considerate, do good follow-up and be attentive…but they hadn't though about points like *move the conversation forward* at the end of every call. There was a lot of Aha! about positioning things. They realized they needed to be consciously thinking: 'How am I moving to the next step?' instead of just hanging up the phone."

According to Carroll, if you are interested in opening the door to a much stronger repeat sale, you need to think about making human connections when you make those 20 Call Bursts. It is one thing to motivate sales people, but if you really want to give them techniques, or tools, 20 Call Bursts are without a doubt the technique that will give you proven results. Carroll adds:

> If you have established a relationship with an individual and yet you are promoting your services to them, it's easier to retain them as a repeat customer if you have that relationship, because it's more personal. Because you are going more down the relationship track, through the up and down of the economy, you get to sustain business and you build a better foundation.

> We don't view what we sell as too different from what others sell. We do sell more of an experience and we are conscious of the environment—or ambiance. Ultimately in our company, I want to get away from the word *sales*. To me, it is more about *connecting*.

ClubCorp. aims to bring people into a private environment that will help their relationships and their businesses grow. The longer someone is a part of this experience, the more valuable that experience becomes. If you belong to a private club, even something as small-scale as a local gym, you know what Carroll is talking about. You go to mingle with others who go to the same club or gym; you go to establish connections with those people; and you might go to generate business or better networking connections. For the sales force at ClubCorp., they try to sell their clubs based on this idea. As Carroll says:

> I feel that we definitely raised the consciousness of having our folks look at their sales process differently. I feel wholeheartedly that we are asking more in-depth questions, and more people are thinking about moving conversations forward. Let's say someone has already booked an event, such as a business breakfast meeting. Our people are doing a better job at increasing or maximizing the conversation to move it towards "What can we do next?"

ClubCorp. was affected by September 11, 2001, as were many others in business. It operated the Metropolitan Club in Chicago's Sears Tower and had to pay particular attention to those clients. But because the company had already been practicing the *move the conversation forward* approach, it was able to best deal with challenges that followed that event. ClubCorp. kept moving forward and continued to keep conversations going forward through the roughest of roads, which allowed the company to stay focused. "If you did not have the attitude to keep moving, many companies that have not used the *move the conversation forward* approach…probably recovered more slowly."

Also key to ClubCorp.'s new take on selling was acknowledging that the relationship was more important than the transaction. Carroll articulates:

> It does not mean that every phone call should result in a transaction. It is not a rejection if you did not book a new event, party or

sale. We are more focused on *"What did you do in that conversation to build the relationship?"*; *"What did you learn about that individual?"*; or *"How were you able to know when you could call them again or when there might be another opportunity?"*

Ask yourself these questions the next time you finish a round of 20 Call Bursts. If you can answer these easily and with promising results, you'll be well on your way to moving more sales conversations forward. In addition to asking the right questions to find the right connection with people, the initial approach to your calls is equally important. And this is when working through your call lists is vital.

Working Through Lists

Another company, Bartsch, Trotter Associates, deserves some attention because it also has implemented the concepts discussed in this book and has seen results. The marketing communications company is owned and operated by Sandra Bartsch and Charles Trotter, and is based in Los Angeles, California. Among their clients are Mercedes Benz and the Democratic National Convention Committee. The events and marketing tools they create for companies are sweeping in scope, expensive…and powerful. When I interviewed them about how went about making calls and moving conversations forward, the importance of call lists in their day came up.

As Bartsch notes:

I personally use two separate call lists. I use a call book and a day-at-a-glance book. The day-at-a-glance book is basically a calendar. I use it to write down what calls I need to make on a given day. The other book is a record of which calls I make, and if there is a call that I have to make at another day, I put it into the day-at-a-glance on the day I need to call them back.

Bartsch uses a master list of calls and another that is an actual description and record of who she has to call on what day and what she needs to talk to the target about. This has worked well for her and her business. "Obviously, I have to be very disciplined and write everything down," Bartsch admits. She adds:

When I open the book on a specific day, and there are several people or companies I am looking forward to talking to, the great thing is that I work through the list. I don't cherry pick. I start at the top and work my way down. …What's funny is that I know where people are, when they are returning, and I can talk to them about that. I can ask questions about their trips out of town.

According to Charles Trotter, "There are steps to our process." He made some changes to his process through working with me and has seen a difference in the way people respond to him and his sales pitches:

A huge breakthrough for me was that I was not calling to close the deal. The concept of moving the conversation forward really freed me from the pressure of trying to make something happen on every single phone call. We call on a wide range of organizations, some of which are huge. For me, being tied to the outcome of a "yes" or "no" was troubling. If things ended up in a "no," I viewed it as a failure. What happened was that every call was a "no" because of who I was being when I was calling them. I was attached to having them buy something.

Through the work we did, Trotter came to realize that what he sold couldn't be bought in a single phone call. "I wasn't even aware that it couldn't be bought in a single phone call!" he told me. He admits:

Move the Sale Forward

We provide corporate communications company that produces live events and meetings. Our average sales cycle (cold intro to actual event) is anywhere from one to two years. Our business is really based on trust. You cannot buy something from us, and if you don't like it, send it back. There is no guarantee that it will go well, that it will succeed. If you go into business with us, or get into bed with us, there is only our reputation for you to make your decision based on.

This makes maintaining not only conversations—but a reputation—a priority for Bartsch and Trotter. According to Bartsch, learning how to better communicate with prospects and clients on the phone had an impact on their business, giving them both a renewed sense of confidence. They redefined what the word *communication* means when it comes to the telephone. "The work that *moving the conversation forward* does for me is shifts the whole process to me being a powerful listener—and not a powerful talker," Bartsch says. She also adds:

You are countering the common view. For the person who is receiving the telephone call, you're dispelling the common notion of what someone who makes a business introduction over the telephone is. You are not in sales when you call someone. Sales communication to me, as a result of working through this process, is helping me to change the expectation of the person on the other side, to shifting the whole dynamic.

Once Bartsch began to implement the concepts underlying *moving the conversation forward* approach, she began to have powerful interactions over the phone and saw how both parties got something out of it. She and Trotter also noted how people will tell you things over the phone that they would never say when you're face to face. As soon as they started to focus on listening rather than talking, they learned a lot more about their customers. They also discovered how much they didn't need to talk or worry about filling every silent moment. Bartsch remarks:

> I have certainly noticed when I am talking too much. I feel that I need to get the other person talking. There might be a quick pause in the conversation, and I can now let a pause happen in a conversation and not feel as though I need to fill the space. I guess I feel more confident now, that I do not have to fill every second of space with me talking. I have lived in then US for five years now. I was raised in Germany and I think people definitely respond to each other differently.

In developing a process to their selling, Bartsch and Trotter gained a great deal of confidence that helped them further hone their techniques and better respond to prospects and clients. Their story serves as a testament to the value of planning your calls and following through your lists by being a powerful listener.

Conclusion

Moving sales conversations forward is an emotional and intellectual enterprise. Not 30 minutes before I sat down to work on this section, did I get off the phone with a client we started doing business with this year.

It took me over seven months to get a face-to-face meeting with this particular client and that meeting went very well. They decided to give me a shot at a project and before the project was completed they booked me for more work.

The conversation started taking on a life of its own, and it took almost as much effort for me to *not* sell to them, yet stay in front of them. I wanted to close more business but not appear greedy, and so on and so on. It boils down to the simplistic miracle of not deciding in advance what should happen, but being open and patient enough to find out what *can* happen.

Some conversations should simply aim to check the progress of your performance. Those calls can end with an invitation for you to attend a special managers' meeting in order to find out how you can work together in the coming months.

Enthusiasm and patience working together may sound like a tall order, but consider this: People are not sitting at their desk, nor out attending classes trying to figure out how to get rid of sales people. You probably don't like the feeling that you are being sold, so why should we expect that the people we call on to be any different? We hit roadblocks, speed bumps and sales conversation gridlock more often due to our own lack of skill and preparation than for any other reason.

No matter the amount of enthusiasm you have, you must skillfully use it to move conversations forward. In addition, if your prospect answers your questions and does not qualify, don't assume he is being difficult. Either you are asking the wrong questions or you're trying to sell to the wrong person or company.

You might wonder, "How many times should I call on people without a result before I decide they are a waste of my time?"

The minute you approach someone with the intent of determining if he is a waste of time, you have soured the potential of that relationship. You need to emotionally and mentally shift how you approach secretaries and receptionists; move away from the bullying (i.e., "let me through because I'm important") and try another approach (i.e., "I see you as a decision maker and will act and respond accordingly"). This is challenging because it can be hard to hide the sense of urgency you have inside to get to the person you really want to talk on the phone. This is not because sellers aren't good actors. It's because in the business world, people are short on time and bombarded with distractions. People want to get to the point quickly.

Your call and demeanor are consciously (and subconsciously) evaluated at almost a beat-by-beat pace. Check your attitude. Gauge and shore up your enthusiasm. Qualify people based on your specific criteria.

My specific criteria has as much to do with the *human* I am speaking with as it does with the number of locations she manages or the average dollar amount of the potential sale.

So—how many times should you call before you decide they might be a waste of time? If you want a specific number, I can't help you.

If your goal is to connect with people, and you realize that it won't happen with everyone, then you are ready to move many, many sales conversations forward.

Now that we've covered basic sales conversations, we can take the lessons further and talk about moving sales *management* conversations forward, which is the focus of Chapter 6.

Move the Sale Forward

Chapter 7:
Killer Questions

The questions you ask make a huge difference in the responses you get and are elemental in establishing and maintaining relationships. You can ask a bunch of questions, hopscotching around without a distinct objective, which frustrates the people involved. You can also fire off a steady stream of pointed, specific questions and be perceived as an interrogator.

Or you can think about (and practice) asking questions that go beyond the standard sales approach. Questions that are beautiful in their simplicity, yet absolutely on-target in their ability to get to the heart of the matter. These are killer questions because they take the standard open-ended question to the next level.

To reach the next level, keep the following goals in mind when formulating your questions:

- I want the other person to start talking;

- I want my question to put the other person at ease; and

- I want my question to be focused on the other person and their business, as opposed to me, my product or service, or how I think they should act, think or respond.

Over the years, it has become clear to me that we all tend to ask yes/no questions. "Yes" and "no" are, after all, among the first words we learn as children. We also have a tendency to pose questions that lead to a "no." If someone asks you yes/no questions, chances are you'll say "no," and there are a few reasons for that.

First, you'll tend to say "no" because it's easy. You don't have to make any commitments and can go on with your life.

So, since you want to be more successful in moving conversations forward, the one thing you want to avoid are yes/no questions, replacing them instead with open-ended questions. Then you can build upon and improve your open-ended killer questions, which follow a logical progression of thought and keep a laser focus on the issues.

These questions move the conversation forward. They require more than a "yes" or "no" response. They are short, pointed and about the other person.

Open-ended killer questions position the customer or prospect as the decision maker and the driver in each and every conversation. They require you to apply good listening skills because the core of your prospect's message must be the key ingredient of the next question.

Some argue that it's a good idea to keep asking questions strictly to get your prospect or customer to keep talking. But I think there's a bit more refinement to it and more to the way people respond and react to sales people.

If all I do is ask you question after question, then I'll be perceived as an interrogator. But, if I ask you questions based upon what you just said to me, I have your attention and you tend to share more with me.

If you can get your prospect to share one detail with you that he doesn't share with your competitor, you set yourself apart. If you repeat that detail back to your prospect later in conversation, and your prospect is surprised that you knew this tidbit, you show your prospect that you actually *listen when he talks.*

That sets you apart as well.

The importance of asking questions designed to keep the conversations flowing cannot be overemphasized. Some of my ability to do that has come at considerable cost.

A Little History

Some years ago, I had a client in the Los Angeles area, for whom I conducted sales training. This was my biggest client at the time. The company had over 150 sales people (that meant a fair amount of work for us). They sold a high-tech product (very cutting edge at the time) and the decision maker (I'll call him Tony) and I got along very well.

They also paid on time—which made training all the more valuable.

At the time, I lived in the High Desert, northeast of Los Angeles. I would drive into LA to do a lot of my seminars, and Tony's office was about a 50-minute drive away.

He managed locations all over Southern California and, conveniently, he lived in the High Desert as well. Once I found this out, I asked if he'd meet me over breakfast at a local eatery when we needed to get together. He agreed easily and we set out on a path that was very good for my business.

We had developed a routine. I'd perform a training seminar at one of his locations and we'd get together for breakfast about three business days after and go over the reviews. I'd ask participants to fill out evaluation questionnaires at the conclusion of the session and he and I would review them together. At that time, I had an opportunity to be face-to-face with him (always a good thing).

Move the Sale Forward

I'd present him with the evaluations from the session and ask him, "What would you like me to do next?"

Usually, he'd want me to go to another office within two to three weeks and train another group. He was a great client; every time I did some work for him, he'd reward me with more work.

Tony had a cellular phone that he loved to use. He used it almost all the time. After the first few times I called his office and his secretary offered to give me his cell phone number, I realized that it might not be considered a breach of protocol for me to call him on his cell phone. I reluctantly dialed the number. He answered and was glad to hear from me. I asked him how comfortable he was with me calling him on the cell phone in the future.

"I always have it on, John—so it's probably better for you to try me on it, than at the phone in the office."

Okay, I thought. I'd continue to call him that way in the future. About a week later, I completed the assigned training session for his group. I wanted to set the next breakfast meeting with Tony, so I excitedly dialed. He answered. We began the discussion. Suddenly, I heard this unique loud screech through the phone. It was in the background of wherever he was. I was curious, so I asked: "Where are you?"

Without missing a beat, and without a hint of humor, Tony replied, "What have you got on your mind?" To say that there was anything menacing in his voice would be overdramatizing things. I was certainly caught off guard, though. I didn't know what to say. I stuttered for what felt like an eternity and he offered no help. He wouldn't let me off the hook.

His current location had nothing to do with our business. I was at fault because I had brought it into the conversation. He let me just hang there on a limb. Finally, I tried to make light of what he had said. "I don't have anything in mind…I just was wondering… ." I trailed off and realized that I was just digging a deeper hole—one that he was not going to help me out of.

Once I found a way to end the conversation, we hung up, but not before I had asked for another breakfast meeting, to which he seemed to agree. I say he seemed to agree because he didn't say he wouldn't be there. But, when the day for the meeting came and I arrived at our usual place, he didn't show.

I convinced myself that I had either gotten the time or the date wrong and then I called him later that day on his cell phone. He answered and I asked about the missed meeting. He was vague and unapologetic. I, wanting to move forward, asked for an alternative meeting. He didn't say he wouldn't be there, so I (consumed with desire to get this rolling again) went to the meeting place, on the day I thought we had agreed to.

He didn't show.

Then it hit me. Tony spent a lot of time running all around Southern California. According to him, his cell phone was "always on." By my asking him: "Where are you?" I had, quite innocently, attempted to take the conversation somewhere *it didn't need to go.* This misstep ended the relationship, which created repercussions and a personal lesson I was not eager to repeat.

I learned a few years later, from someone who had also known Tony, that he kept parrots. He had big, loud, screeching birds in his den. When I called him, thanks to the miracle of modern technology, we were carrying on a business conversation, and his location had no bearing on what we were talking about, or any other aspect of our relationship. He was working from home, and he didn't need to share that with me.

We never did business with each other again. I lost the largest account I had at the time.

You might wonder how someone like that stays in business. But the answer to that question doesn't matter. The end (and moral) of the story is this: *Moving conversations forward requires us to maintain our focus and to not attempt to take the relationship somewhere that the other person is not interested in taking it.*

Move the Sale Forward

Look at this from the perspective of maintaining any other type of relationship. If we ask something of the other person too early in the relationship, it can do irreparable damage.

Selling is not easy, but because of its challenges, there are many things that can distract or prevent you from working on and mastering the basics.

Nowhere in this book will you find a list of questions for you to memorize and use. Some select examples are included, but there's no list for you to copy and try on your next sales call. And there's a reason for this.

I don't sell what you sell, in the environment that you sell. Only you, your manager and your colleagues can work with you to develop the questions you need to apply to your unique selling situation. And as soon as you get comfortable with a specific list, it's time to build new ones.

Developing new questions on a regular basis will lead you to being more comfortable thinking and responding.

The list to the left shows you the words that will lead you to formulating an open-ended question, when placed near the beginning of the question. If you begin with one of the words from the list on the right (closed), you're setting yourself up for a "yes" or "no" answer (most likely a "no"). You don't want to get a "yes" or "no" answer. Why? Because it limits or ends the conversation.

Open-ended (Do's)	Closed (Don'ts)
Who	Is
What	Can
When	Will
Where	Do

<u>Open-ended (Do's)</u>	<u>Closed (Don'ts)</u>
Why	**Does**
How	**Could, Would, Should**
Which	**Has, Have**
	If
	Are

Since "no" is negative and "yes" provides you with virtually no information, you want to use open-ended questions to dig a bit deeper. Answers to these questions will help you to learn what's on people's minds, which will lead you to the next component or building block of open-ended questions—emotion.

People buy based on emotion. Knowing this, you must uncover what's in people's hearts and heads in order for you to move the conversation forward.

Emotional Triggers

Incorporate emotional triggers into the questions you ask to help you dig deeper. Examples of emotional trigger words include: *like*, *want*, *feel*, *think*, *believe*, *understand*, *agree*, *enjoy*, *hope*, *love* and *help*.

You may have one or two words you would like to add to the above list of emotional triggers. Keep in mind that these words are tools to really get people talking. When you get someone talking, you are obligated, as a professional (and as a human being) to listen to what the person has to say.

To that end, understand that, when you ask a question, be prepared to listen to the answer. It may take time and it may require patience. When you ask a question, be prepared to listen—fully—to the answer.

The last emotional trigger on our list here—help—is particularly important. Help is what we all need, what we all are more than happy to offer, but what we tend to be reluctant to ask for.

Why are we reluctant to ask for help? Too often, we feel as though there's a danger in our appearing weak or that we don't know what we're talking about. This makes all the difference in the *move the sale forward* philosophy and here's why: The more you tell someone what you know, the less likely that person will want to engage in conversation with you.

The more you begin sentences with the word "I," the less interested your prospect will be in continuing the conversation. Don't sound like a know-it-all when it comes to your prospect's needs and wants.

☞ **Point of Impact #6:** The third time you begin a sentence with the word "I" is when your listener loses interest.

Some sales people begin their cold calls with statements like: "I know your company is planning _____ and I was calling to share with you how we could help." This sounds strong and it certainly has worked for some, otherwise people would not continue to implement it. But it assumes too much and can alienate your prospect. Right away, your prospect is told up front that you know about his future plans and that *you* think you can help him.

My challenge to you is to develop an opening statement that points toward moving the conversation forward, as opposed to wrestling the sale away. Get your prospect to think *he* needs your help, rather that you telling him that blankly.

Since we are addressing the emotional aspect of selling, we must also address what usually goes on emotionally for the salesperson as the conversation progresses.

If you make your living by earning commission, when you feel a commission is imminent, you get excited. You may even feel a surge of energy, prompting you to react to what is going on. But don't forget about Point of Impact #4: The appropriate time to celebrate a sale is after the commission check clears your bank.

I repeat this Point of Impact because a wide range of emotions constantly beleaguers sales people. In my experience, I felt a greater sense of control over the selling process once I learned to work to keep my emotions and manage my selling, my income and my stress level on an even keel.

Also, Point of Impact #3 begs to be reiterated: The best way to direct a conversation is to keep emotion out of it.

This is an enormous challenge. How do you balance your use of emotional trigger words while keeping emotion out of it? And, if people buy based on emotion, then how can you keep emotions out of it?

As I mentioned before, if you've ever been in a relationship, you've probably experienced conflict. When you became emotionally involved in resolving that conflict, you lost two things probably: perspective and control. Many sales people say that the best way for them to close a deal is to act as if they don't care if the deal closes or not. There is some validity to that. As soon as it becomes apparent to the buyer that you have a great emotional stake in the specific transaction, you lose your negotiating edge. You lose your position of power. You lose your ability to direct the conversation.

So (to reiterate), your goals are to:

1) Direct the conversation;

2) Be persuasive; and

3) Be perceived as non-threatening.

Move the Sale Forward

Once you can achieve all three, you're in a position where the conversation can be about more important and lasting issues than price and delivery. You begin to discuss the best way to maintain the relationship.

To understand better how to ask open-ended killer questions, let's begin by identifying some accepted criteria for these questions. You'll see how these questions compare to the closed-ended questions we grew up asking.

Next, you'll begin to open-ended killer questions by incorporating the building blocks. You'll be able to create your own. And, once you've applied your techniques for formulating open-ended questions for about 30 days, I recommend that you return to the questions you list here and compare them with the responses you received from prospects. Evaluate whether or not they achieved the goal of getting your prospect talking and moving the conversation forward.

> **The best reason to write your questions down is so that you can return in a week, a month or a year to re-evaluate what you've written and be inspired to re-formulate some of them.**

In order to be considered killer questions, they must meet the following criteria:

1) They must be focused;

2) They must be about the prospect/customer;

3) They must be based on what the prospect/customer just said; and

4) They must include either emotional triggers and/or one of the building blocks we will continue to add.

Before you feel overwhelmed, take a deep breath and prepare for the next phase of what we will achieve together. Up to this point, you've probably realized that the whole process we are proposing is more about the way *you* think during the selling conversation than any specific if/then type of methodology.

An if/then methodology is one that finds its answers by laying out a list of possible scenarios. After the list of scenarios, it offers the "reliable" response to that scenario. This methodology is difficult to manage and master. If you can abandon the use of scripts for cold calling, you'll free yourself up for greater possibilities.

Scripts that formulate a presentation style will only lead to disappointment and frustration. You'd spend hours considering possible responses people would give you to the statements or questions you had scripted. With scripts, you'll never find any prospects/customers who have a copy of the same script. Even though you'll encounter similar responses over and over again, you'll never come across the same conversation twice, with questions and responses occurring in the same order.

We've established the building blocks for killer questions—open-ended words like *who, what, when, where, why, how* and *which* and emotional trigger words.

Try to formulate some questions here:

_____

_____

_____

_____

_____

_____

To make sure you are on the right track, let's review the criteria. If any of your questions begin with *are, is, can, will,* etc., then you need to go back and do them again. If you didn't include an emotional trigger, go back. If you feel you've met these criteria and that you went down the right road, now is a perfect time to test these.

Find someone in the office, at home or in the mall and ask him an open-ended question. One thing to keep in mind as a rule of thumb for identifiers is their order:

It's okay to follow a Do word with a Don't word. For example: *What can* we do to earn your business? *When is* a good time for us to connect again?

Another way to put this:

Do's	Don'ts	
What	do...	you think?
When	would...	be the best time to talk again?
How	can...	we move this forward?

When you follow a Do (word) with a Don't (word), it simply gives you a reminder that when you start to ask a question with a closed-ended word, you're starting down the road to a "no" answer, which will not lead to a sale or even an opportunity to move the conversation forward.

If you start with an open-ended word to make an open-ended question, you have a greater chance of getting more information.

Next, you incorporate an emotional trigger, then move forward with words that add some color or zip to the question. Something that sparks the imagination, and creates a more dramatic picture in their minds. These words are called *qualifiers*.

Some sample qualifiers are:

Important	Productive	Efficient	Reasonable
Valuable	Often	Effective	Critical
Useful	Beneficial	Crucial Impact	

Many more words can be qualifiers. Take a minute and add your own words to the qualifier list:

_____   _____

_____   _____

_____   _____

_____   _____

Asking open-ended questions must go beyond the ability to lead someone down a predefined path. Adding qualifiers puts the people we ask questions in a position to think about their situation in a way where they are focused on their concerns and their priorities, as opposed to our offer and our desire to sell.

Now it's your turn to work. Use the tools we've outlined to build some questions of your own, incorporating each of the building blocks presented so far—identifiers, emotional triggers and qualifiers. Don't use any evaluation criteria (i.e., Does it sound business like? Would I respond to that question?) that might disqualify your efforts.

First, recognize this as an exercise. Second, you cannot expect people to respond and think the exact way you do. If you do, you're setting yourself up for disappointment after disappointment. If you don't do the exercise, your thinking will not change and neither will your results. Use the following page as a worksheet for your question-building.

Move the Sale Forward

Your Killer Questions

1)_____?

2)_____?

3)_____?

4)_____?

5)_____?

6)_____?

7)_____?

8)_____?

9)_____?

10)_____?

11)_____?

12)_____?

13)_____?

14)_____?

15)_____?

Check to make sure, in each of your questions, that you:

- Follow a Do with a Don't;
- Use an emotional trigger; and
- Incorporate a qualifier.

Notice the difference in your questions from those you usually hear from sales people, such as:

➡ "Do you want me to stop by?"

➡ "Can we meet next week?"

➡ "Is this something you think you want to do?"

➡ "Can we expect to get an answer soon?"

➡ "Should I fax you an Order Form?"

And the more effective ways of asking:

➡ When would be a good time for me to stop by?

➡ Where can we meet next week?

➡ How can we determine if this is something you want to do?

➡ At which point should I expect an answer?

➡ What kind of material would you like to see from me?

Do your best to stay away from the personal "I." As mentioned before, sales people tend to begin conversations with "I." "I" statements are innocent enough, as far as intent, but they fall short of the mark when positioned and delivered with the intent to make a connection to the listener.

Notice that by virtue of thinking about the questioning process differently, we've changed the fundamental focus of the conversation. When someone asks you what *you* think, you are the focus. On the other hand, when someone asks you when you'll buy, who is the focus? Not you.

 Remember: Your role is to be the navigator. The prospect's or customer's role is to be the driver. Replace "I" with words like "you," "we" and "us" as often as possible.

It's important for you to get a feel for how your questions sound. In addition to sharing your ideas with friends for feedback, call on other sales people who want to develop better skills. Have them tell you how they would react to the questions you've formulated. Everyone will have a different perspective, which will add to your own evolving perspective.

Again, this is an opportunity for dialogue about this process and more importantly, the folks you talk to will be in the driver's seat right off the bat because you're asking them to evaluate something and give you feedback.

Once you've run your questions by these people, make note of their responses. Realize that explaining the intent of a question or approach compromises the purity of the experiment. Practice your listening by simply reading them the question and detailing their response on paper. Try not to filter or evaluate their responses. Take them at face value.

> The point of this exercise is an important one: If you sell (or communicate) based on how you personally would react, you are limiting the scope of your selling skills. Not everyone thinks, feels or reacts the way you do. You need to open yourself up to the various ways in which a person can react, and gather a set of skills that can work on all these different people.

If you say what you think people want to hear, you won't really express yourself. If you evaluate what you're about to say based on what you think another person's potential reaction will be, you're second guessing the impossible. If you ask questions based on a genuine curiosity and desire to help people, you tend to be perceived as more genuine *because you are*.

At this point what do you think is most important for you to find out about people and the way they think? Your answer may be different now than it was when you first started walking through this process. It will probably change again once you have applied what we are discussing.

Action Words

The final building block after do's, don'ts, emotional trigger words and qualifiers for open-ended killer questions are called action verbs. *Action verbs* create or point to some specific action. Action verbs draw people in and get them thinking about the next step.

 Remember: Any forward motion is good. Any next step is good. And any new information is good. When we effectively manage our expectations, we view any response we get from a prospect or customer strictly as information.

Move the Sale Forward

Our killer questions take on a new dimension when we add action verbs. Try a few more questions or add an action verb to the questions you have already built. It's not essential that your questions contain every type of building block; rather, use the building blocks to help generate conversation that takes you and your prospect or buyer forward.

The last thing you want as a result of sharpening your skills is to be so focused on building the "best" question that you miss what someone is saying to you. This is why I encourage you to build a few of these while you are working through this book.

Action verbs include: *solve, avoid, do, evaluate, choose, fix, accomplish, measure, investigate* and *learn*. Adding action verbs to your questions will give them more of a punch.

Now add a few of your own action verbs. Think of words that imply or require thinking, moving, changing or acting:

_____   _____

_____   _____

_____   _____

_____   _____

So let's throw out a few more killer questions, with many of the building blocks in place:

- How valuable would our service be to you?

- What do you want to accomplish with us?

- When do you want to learn more about how our services can help you?

- How much time do you think we have to solve this problem?

- How comfortable are you with us moving forward?

- What are the key criteria you feel are most important in order to evaluate this offer?

- How often can I call you so I'm not a pest and I don't miss an opportunity to help you?

- What is a reasonable expectation, as far as how long I should wait to hear from you?

- What else?

- What would you like to know about us?

- What top three things are impacting your business this year?

In Chapter 2 we covered the story of SureWest, a company that shifted its sales techniques and experienced greater sales by simply focusing on making 20 Call Bursts and being diligent about asking open-ended killer questions.

SureWest changed its approach to serving customers, moving away from the philosophy that the company should fill needs of customers, to the idea of establishing human connections with customers in order to move conversations forward. This, in turn, would bring in new business.

The box on the following page contains sample killer questions that the company has used to generate these human connections. Take a look at these and note how they typify the kinds of questions every seller should ask. Some, as you'll see, have already been mentioned as examples in the book.

A Glance at One Company's Killer Questions

How often may I call you so I'm not a pest and don't miss an opportunity to help you?

What do you think is our best next step?

What is the most important thing you need to know about us, before you would consider working with us?

What would you like to see in the proposal?

What value do you put on your communication?

How does that compare with what you expected?

What can we do to earn your business?

What would need to happen before you would consider us?

What are you unhappy with regarding your current provider?

What would need to happen before it would make sense for you to review your telecommunication services?

What would you like to see improved?

What changes would you like to make?

When you are talking with your boss, what is the most common issue he brings up?

When would you like to finalize this?

What direction do you see this going?

What kind of budget are you working with?

What would you like to see, that would help you make an informed decision instead of just a decision?

> **What should I put together in order to prepare for our next meeting?**
>
> **How should I prepare for that meeting?**
>
> **Who else along with yourself is involved in making that final decision?**
>
> **What do you like about what you are currently using?**
>
> **What are you looking to accomplish in the coming year?**

It's easy to see that every one of the above questions is open-ended. There are no questions that will get a simple "yes" or "no" response. They open the conversation up to greater topics that will hopefully lead to deeper connections and lasting business relationships.

Conclusion

Much of what we've discussed in this chapter boils down to risk. There is a risk in attempting to move a conversation forward through asking open-ended questions as opposed to trying to force the conversation forward with data, convincing arguments or case studies. There is risk in working on an approach that may not come naturally to you. There is risk in going outside of your comfort zone—going outside the framework you had used in the past—to try a new way of thinking. And, as we'll see in the upcoming chapter, there is risk in handling objections, as opposed to delivering a prepared litany of tried and true responses.

This entire book is dedicated to motivating you to take more risks and think through the process. It's about you going somewhere you've never been before professionally.

Move the Sale Forward

Below is another list of sample open-ended killer questions for you to study and think about. Some you'll recognize from previous pages, but see if you can take the key elements of these and reframe them to fit your own selling repertoire.

More Killer Questions

1) When would it be worthwhile for us to speak again?
2) What are your goals for the next year?
3) What was the last deal you did?
4) How do you feel about your current location?
5) What three things can I do to help you?
6) What are the three most important aspects of an opportunity that you focus on?
7) What do you see in your crystal ball?
8) When can we do something?
9) What do we need to do to move forward?
10) What are the most important issues affecting your business?
11) How long have you been here?
12) How does your company make decisions?
13) How can we solve that problem?
14) What would make you more efficient?
15) When do you establish next year's financing?
16) How has the economy affected your business?
17) How has your business grown?
18) How will growth affect your plan?
19) What else?
20) How does that sound?
21) How do you feel about taking the next step?
22) Where do we go from here?
23) What's next?

CHAPTER 8:

HANDLING OBJECTIONS

Objections are a distasteful, yet consistent fact of sales life. Your attitude toward and ability to handle them will have a bearing on your success, but it will not take you all the way toward being successful when they're thrown your way. And they will get thrown your way! We don't want to overcome objections as much as we want to *handle* them. We don't want to react to objections; we want to respond to them.

If we go forward with the assumption that all information is good information, we can view objections as something to handle and respond to, as opposed to something we must defeat on our way to victory.

One additional note regarding the driver/navigator conversation scenario. When you're face to face in a conversation with someone, there's a slight air of confrontation. Your exchange is made up of a call and response scenario. You say something, then the other person says something. The information goes back and forth and it's difficult to make progress because you're both holding your ground and don't want to yield to one another.

Employing the driver/navigator scenario, we have a different perspective. We're looking in the same direction: down the road. We're elbow-to-elbow, shoulder-to-shoulder, moving forward. When the conversation includes the words "we," "us" and "together," it's a cooperative, inclusive affair.

Move the Sale Forward

When we look at objections, we must mentally stay within the driver/navigator analogy. An objection is simply a response that asks for clarification or persuasion.

Traditional sales mentality has fostered phrases as inane as: "No really means 'yes'" or "An objection simply means 'You haven't sold me yet'." To me, objections are expressions of concern or actual reasons for a prospect not to buy. Trying to convince someone to buy my product when it's not right for him or her helps no one. If I want to be persuaded, I don't want to be shown my error in judgment or my lack of education. If I'm comfortable enough to tell you that I don't like a certain aspect of the deal, that issue must be addressed.

For example:

Prospect: "It sounds pretty expensive to me."

Salesperson: "How important is price in your overall decision?"

Not: "Well, your competitor is buying this all the time at this price."

Note that we are keeping a focus on the issues and following a logical progression of thought. You must respond to what the customer just said, yet without judgment, evaluation or emotional stock in the response. Your response should also point to the next step in the conversation: gathering more information.

Prospect: "We don't need anything like that right now."

Salesperson: "When do you think it might make sense for us to talk again?" *Not*: "Oh no? What do you need?" or "When will you need it, so I can call back and get the order?"

Stay focused and logically proceed through conversations based on what others say; avoid emotional involvement.

There are many ways folks will attempt to stop the conversation or see if they can get you to go away. Some people just want to see if they are better at getting you off the phone than you are at keeping them on. It's fun to treat it as if it were a contest.

Let's look at some of the ways that folks stop conversations. You can probably think of quite a list, but the point of this exercise is to develop a technique you can master in order to be more prepared for these responses when you hear them.

> **Your challenge in handling objections is that you're going to avoid stock answers. There is no script that can be written with all of the answers and all of the responses that lead to a sale.**

As a sales professional, you need to be prepared to think on your feet, listen, and respond to what you hear. Here are some objections you might come across:

- "We do that internally."

- "I don't have time right now."

- "We have an existing agreement with a provider."

- "We don't have any more room in the budget."

- "We never pay for a service like that."

- "You need to contact the corporate office."

- "Call me next fiscal year."

Move the Sale Forward

- "He's out of the office, and I don't know when he will return."

- "There's no way the committee would approve that much money."

- "We get a special deal on that from one of our customers."

- "We have never done anything like that."

You get the idea. Maybe the statements of objection you hear are phrased a bit differently, but the messages are similar.

There are really only four ways people try to stop a conversation. I call them The Four True Objections. They are:

- No money;

- No need;

- No hurry; and

- No confidence.

If you focus on handling these four, it will get you farther along in the conversation.

There are some immutable laws we find ourselves dealing with when conversing with others, and regardless of whether or not we like the laws, we're bound by them. One of them is: *People constantly change their minds.* Don't you hate that? You, too, change your mind. You can't let objections to your offers get in the way of your selling.

If a technique you use for landing a new prospect doesn't work, don't turn your back on that technique. It might work on another prospect. I also find that if I give you a technique to handle a specific objection and you encounter the objection, deliver your planned response and don't get the deal, you turn your back on my technique as something that doesn't work.

When handling objections, we must not only be in touch with where our presentation is falling short, we must also prepare for the possibility of our prospects changing their minds about a detail (or three) in between conversations.

As time goes on, people's ideas, perceptions, understandings, priorities and job expectations change. During our process of moving conversations forward, 20 Call Bursts, asking open-ended questions and assuming the position of navigator, we may or will find ourselves returning to a conversation and getting blindsided by the person offering a new and different objection.

As we handle objections, we move through a process that is more than a call and response style of communicating. Prospects and customers have the right to change their minds or have additional questions. They exercise that right whenever they need reassurance or clarification. Your job as a professional seller is to answer any and all questions, regardless of how often they may be asked.

People tend to buy from us for similar reasons, but they have their own way of finding out what they need to learn in order to make the decision to move forward. As part of our overall philosophy of treating each conversation as a singular, unique event, handling objections proves to us that we are doing what we have set out to do: *move forward*.

Take a moment to list some of the objections you have heard in the past week. Where do they fit in our list of four? Which objections did you list that don't fall under one (or more) of these categories?

In order for you to respond to what someone says, you must be able to indicate to that person that you understand. This is where paraphrasing becomes a powerful and useful tool. We never want to "parrot" what the prospect/customer says, but we do want to reiterate the *content* and *intent* of what they've said to us, to ensure understanding.

Once you paraphrase (and confirm that you understand) it's time for you to determine which of these four objections is at the heart of the person's message.

When an objection is presented to us, we tend to want to dissuade the prospect/customer of her opinion. This is human nature. The emotion of the moment kicks into gear and we find ourselves getting excited. We must use discipline and implement the 80/20 principle. We want people to have the right information, especially if their possession of correct information amounts to our securing a commission.

When people tell us what they have heard, or what they believe, and that information is in conflict with what we know to be fact, we get an emotional charge. Since we are talking about a sales conversation and not a family vacation, we have to look at it objectively. As soon as I interrupt someone when they are talking, especially when they are giving me their opinion or stating facts, they are turned off. They feel slighted. In a face-to-face meeting, I do everything I can to show interest by leaning closer to the speaker, looking him in the eye when he speaks (without staring them down) and forcing myself to let him finish.

Often, when I let people get all the way to the end of their thought process, I know whether or not there is a point to continuing the conversation. If I feel that they are convinced they have the best provider for my type of service, I politely try to make my exit. It's fascinating how long people will try to keep you in a meeting when you tell them that you may not be able to help them. They're surprised and possibly nervous that they've made too hasty a decision.

You believe in your product or service and you know it's useful and valuable. You believe that the person you've targeted will benefit by using your product or service. But then the prospect tells you she is not interested or the budget will not allow it, etc. It's an emotional challenge not to give in to the desire to change her mind.

When you feel like someone is trying to change your mind, you probably get impatient with that person. So, instead of trying to change people's minds, lead them through more conversation by paraphrasing what they say to ensure your understanding, and then follow that statement up with an open-ended question that's pointed, short and about them.

The core of the question must be based on what they just said. In the best-case scenario, it should include an emotional trigger and an action verb. When I paraphrase what I have just heard, it gives me a second to make sure that my next question is a good one. And I know it is a good one if it follows the criteria presented earlier. Let's examine each of these four true objections and discuss how to handle them.

No Money

Our choices for handling this objection are straightforward. Since we sell value and people buy based on emotion, we must determine how valuable the prospect feels our product or service is. If their perception of value is preventing the sale, then we must find out what else they would need to learn about our offer in order for it to make sense for them. If current available cash is truly the issue, then we can investigate payment and financing options, or finally, go away.

☞ **Point of Impact #7:** The salesperson who knows when to go away lives to sell another day.

No Need

There are only three options in every sales conversation. They are:

- Identify a need;

- Create interest in an alternative need; or

- Get out.

In order to identify a need, ask open-ended killer questions after delivering a solid introductory statement. There are many people who will tell you that they don't need what you have to offer. A response to this is: "I'm more interested in introducing myself so that down the road, when you look into a service like ours, we might be at the top of your list of possible providers you'd consider."

This won't work every time but it deflates the pressure of: "Here's what I sell. Do you want any or not?" and moves the conversation into a possible future decision. This can also help you create forward motion.

> **If you don't perceive a need, then you must work to create interest in an alternative need. By stepping away from the immediate and having the prospect get into the driver's seat in your conversation, you'll have the opportunity to ask open-ended killer questions to get him talking and allow him to see that your offer may fit into his plan for the future.**

Cold calling is where we hear the objections that stop us in our tracks. Your goal with a cold call should be to get any piece of information you can, from the name of the receptionist, to the name of the decision maker, to an idea of the decision maker's schedule to when their next need may arise.

When I cold call, I often encounter the response that people have already set their training budget for the year. My next question is not about who they have chosen or whether the provider does all the right things. My next question is about the future.

Examples:

➥ How far down the road would you re-evaluate your training options for next year?

➥ What is the most important thing you want to focus on, when you plan training beyond what you are already committed to?

➥ When it's time to look at options for the new year, what would you need to know about us in order for us to be a potential provider?

Note that these questions are not a challenge to their already-made decision. They focus on the next decision. They get people thinking; they also have people examine whether there are gaps in their current service that I might be able to fill.

You don't have to be the sole provider of what you offer to every single client. Look forward to the opportunity to earn the right to ask for more and more business as the relationship develops. You can't make anyone need what you offer, no matter what it is. However, through effective questioning, listening and responding, you may be able to interest them in an alternative they may not have considered. Finally, you may invite yourself out of the conversation, where one of two things will happen as a result:

1) They agree that the timing is bad or you are just not the suitable provider for them; or

Move the Sale Forward

2) They disagree, and will not allow you off the phone until they have asked several questions. It's exciting and satisfying when they ask you to send them some promotional information, in order for them to get a better idea of what you do, how you do it and to see if it will help them.

If after you've identified a need or tried selling an alternative need to a prospect who won't come to an agreement with you, you need to go away.

 Remember: Your timing is not your prospects' or customers' timing. You needing a sale means nothing in their life. Knowing when you need to go away and move on is critical. Don't resort to statements like: "I only need one more sale to win a contest...can you help me out?" Or: "I'm trying to break my sales record from last year...any way you could place an order today?"

Neither of these will attract new customers. Try to ask one question short of being annoying. This may sound facetious or sarcastic, but it's a gut sense you must develop and it's not as difficult as you might think. Their tone, how distracted they sound, the brevity of their answers...all point to our wearing out our customers. By listening well, you can tell when people are distracted or not interested in answering your questions. If that is the case, invite yourself out: "It sounds like this is not the best time for you..." If they agree, ask: "When would be a better time for us to talk?" Any answer they give is a good answer. If it's as simple as: "Try me tomorrow," do exactly that, getting off the phone as quickly and politely as possible.

If the answer is: "I don't think there is anything for us to really talk about. We've seen your product and it just does no work for us." This is my invitation to go away, reset a time in the database for more than four months down the road to call them back, and then politely and quickly get off the phone. I plan the next call this far out on the calendar because I know I can count on the fact that things change.

Facing the realities of life require you to know when to stop. This translates to knowing when to stop eating, knowing when to stop annoying your spouse…and knowing when to end the sales conversation.

No Hurry

In many ways, this is the easiest objection to handle. People buy according to their timing. As a salesperson, you're likely to come into various business situations at odd or imperfect times. That's okay. The point of moving the sale forward is to adapt to the prospect's circumstances…including where they are in their business cycle.

When a prospect says he or she doesn't need what you're selling now…that's an invitation to schedule the last call.

If you can make a genuine appeal to their sense of loss by creating urgency (i.e., the price will go up, this may not be available at a later date, etc.) you'll know that you've tried your best. Don't create a false sense of urgency if it makes you feel uncomfortable. If now is not the time, now is not the time.

No Confidence

Many expressions of doubt can fall under the no confidence heading. We have a few options in handling these various objections.

Move the Sale Forward

First, if someone has had a negative experience with your company, product or industry, prior to getting them to answer your open-ended killer questions you need to hear them out or let them vent. Great customer service is provided to dissatisfied customers, simply by allowing them to get what they are unhappy about off their chest. Once people have the opportunity to vent, they almost start to apologize for being so upset or for reacting the way they did.

If someone tells you he was unhappy the last time he did business with your company, and you don't ask: "What happened?" he'll never let you in.

Second, you must make the most of those good relationships you've spent time developing and ask for testimonial letters. It's amazing how effective these are when someone is nearing a decision and you can provide a testimonial so she can see, learn and hear more about you.

Third, and most complicated, is the famous *Feel/Felt/Found* approach. I call it famous because many people have used this for many years and no one is really sure where it came from. The challenge to you, however, is to use this approach in a particular way so you remain focused on your prospect. You don't want to use it to pressure someone into buying.

Take a look at the ill-used way: "I understand how you feel, because I felt the same way, but I found that.... So, don't you want to go ahead?" Instead, try something like: "I can appreciate how you feel, because I've spoken with others who've felt the same way. What they found, though was that_____. Based on that, what would you like to do?"

The word "appreciate" indicates that you recognize and validate their emotional response, without sounding as though you agree or share that response. It differs also in that you are comparing their findings with other people who've had to make a similar decision, as opposed to telling them what you've experienced or what you think they should do.

Remember: Handling objections is a skill within itself. It requires practice and attention to detail. Most importantly, it requires the best you have to offer as far as patience, intelligence, listening and determination to move the conversation forward.

Here is another big mistake sales professionals make: When a deal falls through, for whatever reason, they walk away, dejected. If unanswered questions still remain (and you feel that you wouldn't risk losing any future opportunities), you can call the person back and ask her what you might have done differently to earn her business.

Note: This is not a ploy to get people to change their minds. It doesn't usually result in your ultimately doing business. It does, however, teach you more about the way people think.

☞ **Point of Impact #8**: If you have nothing and you risk that nothing and lose that nothing, you've lost nothing. But if you don't risk anything, you won't win anything, either.

When a call doesn't go well, we tend to be reluctant to call that person back. A great way to jump-start a conversation that didn't go as well as expected is to say: "I've been thinking about our conversation and wondered if I could ask you one more question."

When you hear that someone (regardless of who) has been thinking about you, how does that make you feel? It makes you feel great. To know that you are on someone's mind other than when you're right in front of him or her is very flattering.

Conclusion

Being a successful professional seller means having to face rejection once in a while. You may even face periods in which you experience lots of rejection; this is when you'll need to go farther within yourself to keep your enthusiasm and drive forward. You'll need to recognize that rejection is part of the profession—as it's part of every profession. But, the more rejection you face, the easier it will become to manage objections and find new ways to meet people's needs.

In our next and final chapter, we'll sum up our discussion by talking about the three questions every salesperson must answer. These questions will ensure that you're focused on the right goals, objectives and vision.

Chapter 9:
Three Questions
that Close

The whole point of moving the sale forward is that, if you open strongly and stay persistent, sales will just about close themselves.

Well, *just about*.

Of course, some deals simply need to be closed. Every employee in today's business environment is expected to make a direct positive impact on his or her company's bottom line. Sales professionals have been evaluated using these criteria for centuries. How can you ensure that you're focused on the right goals, objectives and vision? One way is for you to articulate simple, direct and personally meaningful answers to the following three questions:

- What do you sell?

- Who do you sell it to?

- Why should people buy from you?

When someone asks you what you sell, how do you answer? Some of us will say (correctly) that we sell "service." Others (also correct) will say we sell "solutions." These all add up to the one thing everyone sells, which is *value*. So who determines the value of what you sell?

Move the Sale Forward

Value is not determined by how hard the work is or what last year's rate card reflects. The value of your offer is determined on a daily basis by your buying customers—not your competition or your uncooperative prospects and certainly not by how much business you wrote last year. So what's the bottom line? The more people you interact with, (and who feel deeply that you've helped them) the more business you'll generate.

Who do you sell it to? In my experience when someone says that he sells to everyone, he pretty much ends up selling to no one. If your target/ ideal/potential client is not specifically described and identified, then you're shooting all over the map. You must have a specific idea of who your customers are and will be.

I certainly don't expect you to be able to identify who specifically will buy from you (too bad we can't project that with certainty) but you must have qualifying criteria to use, to identify whom to sell to. You won't close every deal. This is a reasonable—not pessimistic—expectation. In addition, you'll probably lose customers for one reason or another. All the more reason to be able to answer the question: Who do you sell to? You must have an idea of who could or might buy from you. These qualifying criteria must include specific addresses, phone numbers and other details you find essential to qualify them. Our definition of *qualify* is: To meet specific criteria.

No one can set your criteria. I can help you set those criteria, however, by making sure that you clearly iden-tify common characteristics among the people you sell to now and the people you want to sell to in the future.

Creating new business is a tremendous challenge. There's the poten-tial for us to want that new customer so badly that when the end of the month comes (and it's crunch time to make quota), we're willing to accept someone who doesn't fit our qualifying characteristics. There are times when we are more interested in the transaction than we are in maintaining rate/price/quote integrity. It's tempting—and sometimes easy—to cave and give in when asked for "better pricing" but keep in mind that each time you make a concession, you are opening the door to more concessions and setting a precedent.

Don't fall into the "give in at the last minute to get the deal" trap. Establish the specific criteria for your potential customers and stick to them. *Who are they? What industry are they most often in? What is their level of professionalism? How do they make their decisions? What is their growth potential as a client?*

Let's walk through two of the questions with which we began this chapter:

➡ *What do you sell?*—We sell value, and our client determines the value of what we sell;

➡ *Who do we sell it to?*—We sell the value of our service to a group of clients who meet specific criteria.

Now for the third question:

➡ *Why should they buy it from you?*—The emphasis on the *you* in this question is essential. The answer to this question is the cornerstone of your ability to set yourself apart from the competition.

The best marketing material, the longest amount of time in the business, or an impressive list of clients may not be enough to motivate someone to buy from you. In reality, it rarely is.

If you are new to the selling profession, don't worry if you can't claim any clients as your own. Maybe your company has done business with major companies and you've been instructed to drop the name to build credibility.

I am not discounting that, but make sure that you focus on who *you* are and what *you* can bring to the table. A lack of experience can certainly be viewed as a potential stumbling block toward gaining their acceptance, but don't add to the challenge by seeing yourself as unworthy or not experienced enough.

Who you are counts for a lot, and although naming names may increase the comfort level of the prospect, it is not required in order for you to make a connection with them. If you rely on your ability to get someone else talking, instead of trying to impress that person, you have a greater opportunity to set yourself apart. You can then go get help with the details of getting the deal done from a more experienced person.

> If you are an entrepreneur or an independent contractor (not an employee, so you may not have a lot of help around), you have already taken a considerable risk and should have some support network that can walk you through those things you need help with.

Finally, if you are an experienced seller, and are thinking "I drop names because they give me credibility," I encourage you to renew your enthusiasm for the process by seeing how far you can get into a conversation without mentioning who you have helped before, and instead focus on how you might be able to help this person now.

I have names of clients that are highlighted in my promotional material, as well as on my Web site. Some of them are quoted here in this book. But I don't use them as the card I play to gain entry. I use them when someone asks me: "So who have you worked with, that I might be familiar with?" The beauty of arriving at this question is that it is an unequivocal buy sign. It does not mean that the person *will* buy—it means that he or she is interested in continuing the conversation.

People want to buy from someone they feel right about, someone in whom they have a high degree of trust, confidence and comfort. Doing business implies a relationship, a transfer or exchange of trust, and a transfer of value.

When people pay you or your company, they trade the value of the money for the value of what you offer. The people who buy from you more than once reinforce the fact that they have that trust in you.

One way to get someone to feel this way is by asking him questions focused on the two most fascinating things in his life: himself and his business. The more you listen to what he has to say, the more fascinating he will find you. This is an amazing, reliable and an enduring fact of human nature.

When you ask questions to get a prospect talking about his business, how he solves problems and what would need to happen before he would be interested in doing business with you, you learn more. As a result, he's much more comfortable speaking with you. More importantly, he'll start mentally buying from you.

The questions you ask determine the tone and the direction of any given conversation. You must view the conversation as a strategic step toward achieving a reasonable and attainable goal—to move the conversation forward. In Chapter 1, we talked about how sales people feel compelled to educate their prospects by telling them facts, figures and reasons why the customer should buy from them.

Let's look at this logically. You will introduce yourself, your company, and your offer, and by using the five call objectives (sell, gather information, share information, establish relationships and maintain them), you should be able to determine if your prospect has a "perceived" need for what you're offering.

A perceived need is as important as a real need because chances are your prospect will not buy something from you because *you* think it's a good idea. He'll buy something because *he* thinks it's a good idea. (See Point of Impact #1.)

> The five call objectives walk us through a checklist. The killer question building blocks allow us to use our listening skills to offer a response that the customer finds meaningful.

If your prospect tells you that he doesn't need what you have to offer, your job is not to convince him otherwise. Rather, it's to learn more and see if you might be able to interest him in an alternative need. If you can create interest, then you've shown some flexibility and you've set yourself apart from other sellers. Said more succinctly: Selling is not telling.

The Three-Point Business Plan

Thus far, we've focused on how to sell. We've also addressed activities that are going to impact our comfort level, how we think and how we perform.

With these concepts in our back pocket, let's now turn our attention to where the activity, the mental challenge and the new disciplines we are collecting will take us.

> When you consider your workday, one consistent experience you and I have over time is a sense of needing to

operate in panic mode. Prioritizing, long-range goals
and short-term expectations go out the window at times
without warning. We can get rattled sometimes and
lose focus.

Once you recognize the emotional and psychological rocking of the boat (which can be caused by events as inconsequential as a cancelled appointment or as large as a deal falling apart at the last minute) you can deal with it by taking a look at a three-point business plan.

Now let's look farther down the road at making short and long term plans that work together harmoniously. The simple business plan we'll discuss is one I have used and shared with sales people and sales managers around the country.

When planning your calendar year and establishing what you really want to accomplish, develop a document with long-term goals. Write things down and commit to them.

Regardless of what you sell, whether it's heavy equipment or fractional jet ownership, planning and achieving requires specific measurements. I refer to these as "the numbers." The numbers could, as an example, represent:

1) New accounts;

2) Dollars sold; and

3) Percentage of growth over the previous month or year.

One of my longest client relationships is with GBH Distributing, the company from Chapter 5 that sells headsets, audio and video conferencing tools. The commission structure for its sales people is based on both total dollars sold and gross profit on the number of items sold for each month, quarter and year.

But several of the sales people in this company have their own numbers that motivate them. One wants to be the number one, top seller every month, regardless of how many hours he must put in or cold calls he must make. Another takes great pride in the tenure he has enjoyed with the company and the fact that every client he now works with can be confident that he'll be there next week and next year.

It's a good practice to set goals based on days you'll sell on your calendar. The more days on the calendar you sell, the more you can plan the budget for your business, plan time off, and plan in general so you continue to grow.

Your numbers must be viewed separate from any specific client. My goals, for example, are to begin the selling year with goals for a certain number of:

- New accounts;

- Dates on the calendar;

- Tapes and training products; and

- Books sold.

For all of us, the numbers for this year should be a bit higher than last year because one thing that sales people have in common with athletes is that if we don't continue to stretch ourselves, we lose our competitive edge. Sometimes we lose our ability to stay in the game at all.

For me, being self-employed means I took a great risk on behalf of my family by opening my own business. We've been blessed, in that we were profitable almost from the outset. Over the ensuing two years, our income increased fourfold. And then I got to a point in the development and life of my business where I stopped setting goals. I didn't build a new, updated plan like the one we are going to walk through in this section. This was not a conscious decision to abandon my own advice. I was caught up in the flow of travel, selling, cold calling, mailing, meetings, more cold calling and so on. All of a sudden, I looked at my calendar and it was empty.

My most profitable inventory are days on the calendar. Other folks who sell intangibles or non-essential products and services (i.e., hotel rooms, cruises and others) have this in common with me. The days I have marked on the calendar indicate sold inventory.

The days that are not marked off on the calendar with a client name and a city are days I must spend booking more days. (When you do not have work, your job is to find work.)

It can be a vicious cycle but I absolutely love it. My business requires the best I have to offer, 100 percent of the time. When motivation, productivity, efficiency or revenue is down, it all rests on my shoulders. I can easily go into panic mode when I turn to my calendar and find a void. I face the fact that at some point, I have dropped the ball.

I then have to convince myself that networking and making my usual calls will keep the business going. But in the same way that a bicycle will stop and fall over when no one is pedaling, the momentum of my business can slow down dramatically under my neglect.

This is frightening because my business has a sales cycle of anywhere from four weeks to 10 months. That means that if I don't have any clients in the pipeline, I'm in deep trouble. These minor panic attacks are great wake-up calls for me. I realize the truth of the old adage: If you fail to plan, you plan to fail.

Move the Sale Forward

> *Remember:* A sales cycle describes the amount of time elapsed between initial contact with a prospect, and his cutting a check to purchase or hire. Some people will lessen or increase their perception of a sales cycle based on whether they choose to include competitive biding scenarios.

The time between my first conversation with a decision maker to closing a deal is, on average, three months. Thankfully, our business did not fail as a result but I felt that I had let myself down by not growing the business as aggressively (or consistently) as I should have.

This was not about guilt. It was about missed opportunity. Business was probably out there for me to win, but because I didn't make it enough of a priority, it just didn't happen.

> If you own a hamburger stand that is 100 yards off the freeway, you probably have a lot of opportunity to bring in customers. However, if you don't put up a sign near the freeway, pointing to your business—regardless of whether you have a good product to sell—people will drive by, never even knowing about you, your business or your great burgers.

You probably offer something a bit more sophisticated than burgers—but the analogy stands. You needed to get the word out to people. However well you deliver your product or service, it's virtually worthless if no one knows about it. Having a good reputation in a particular market is the best kind of advertising; once you establish yourself as an honest, reliable seller (with an honest, reliable service or product), people will spread the word and new people will be able to find you.

But none of this happens without effort on your part. You must make the initial connections.

Back to my story of when I had no leads in the pipeline, I had to sit back and look at the calendar over the course of a few days. I thought about how I had filled it before. I thought about who to call who would sympathize and listen to my "poor me" story. I abandoned that idea quickly. No one cared.

I decided to write a plan for activity, with set goals, for the next 90 days, and I implemented the beginnings of the plan the following day. The results were comforting and startling at the same time.

I set a goal of adding 30 new dates to my calendar and I gave myself a deadline of 90 days to accomplish this goal. I allowed myself a reasonable expectation—the proviso that the new dates need only be booked (committed to) and not fulfilled during the 90-day period. I just needed to have a signed contract or a commitment from a client.

I kicked my activity into high gear. I started getting up an hour earlier and staying at the office a half hour later than I had been. I talked to people who were not clients or prospects and told them about my goal. I wrote my goal down. I wrote it on the top of every page in my personal calendar. I wrote it on a big piece of flip-chart paper and posted that on the back of the door that faced my desk.

Every time I left the office, I saw it. Once I got things going again (and it was clear that having specific goals was applicable regardless of where I was in the selling process) I soon had multiple dates on the calendar with several pending. Each time I booked a date, I took a Post-it note, wrote the date I closed the deal, the company, and the date of the engagement on it and posted it to the large piece of flip-chart paper. It allowed me to count backwards, toward the goal of 30 new dates.

Move the Sale Forward

Not only did this give me a constant reminder of the goal, but it also showed me my progress.

It all stemmed from and confirmed my ability to rely on the three-point business plan, which consists of the following:

➡ Targets;

➡ Tactics; and

➡ Time.

Earlier, when we discussed the eight elements to professional selling, we mentioned (as part of our discussion on organization) that knowing whom we were going to call on each day was essential to selling consistently and effectively. The three-point business plan puts this into action.

I had to have an idea of who to call to get my 30 dates booked in 90 days. I couldn't just work though the Yellow Pages or call whomever I found on the Internet who might qualify as a prospect. I had to review my database and think about the different markets I had already tapped.

> **Do some research, get detailed information and get it done quickly. Some sales people prepare for a single phone call by reading every detail on a company's Web site, then hunting around even more for possible news stories or press releases they could mention when they call the prospect. After many minutes of preparation the salesperson will dial, ask for the decision maker by name, and be sent to voice mail. Talk about over preparing!**

Just Get Busy Calling!

Be careful not to over-prepare. There are a few reasons why you should limit the amount of research and preparation you go through prior to picking up the phone or walking into an office of a prospect.

First, you may experience the scenario described above. A bunch of facts gathered, a lot of mental gymnastics, all to have the wind taken out of your sails because the prospect isn't answering the phone, or in the office.

Second, you knowing more about the prospect helps (but does not guarantee) that you will get him or her talking.

Third, and most importantly, nothing takes the place of activity. *Nothing.*

We begin our three-point business plan by looking at targets. We must start with a general goal of who our targets should be (i.e., software companies within 45 miles of the office) to see if they qualify as leads or prospects.

In the next part of our business plan we'll look at tactics.

Get to Work

Pull out a piece of blank paper and get creative. Write these questions across the top: What can we do in addition to cold calling? Are there networking events? Are there trade shows? Publications? Associations? Determine your markets with great care.

Once you determine your market, look for so-called "watering holes." These are the places and events where the folks in this market gather. Whether they gather to see each other, to look for business, to promote their business—this is where you need to go. Anywhere that you know several people in a specific market (or related groups of markets) will gather is a good place to make sure you gather with them.

Move the Sale Forward

An example of a defined market would be the staffing industry. Companies that provide temporary, payrolled help to businesses. The American Staffing Association tells me that companies in their industry (members and non-members) operate in a $6 billion per year business. This indicates to me that these companies are generating revenue, will most likely have a sales force and can meet some of my qualifying criteria as a target. My experience tells me that they must compete on a different level than just price, and the membership search window on The American Staffing Association's Web site (staffingtoday.net) tells me there are many companies who are involved, locally, regionally and nationally.

I tend to start to identify a specific market via their associations. Virtually every vertical market has an association, many with local chapters. It does not cost a lot (comparatively) to go to a meeting as a guest and learn about how that association serves, communicates to and connects with their members.

> **A quick search on the Internet for associations in general, or associations for a vertical market you identify, can yield some surprising (and satisfying) results.**

Once you identify the watering holes—the meetings, the trade shows and the publications—you must determine your tactics for getting in front of those decisions makers. There are several ways of doing this. Your goal is to get your name, company name and product or service in front of people.

Pay attention also to the various industry-specific magazines, newsletters, online portals and business publications out there. Think about contributing to one or two of them editorially. It can help your career as a sales professional and expose your business to hundreds—sometimes thousands—of other businesses.

Remember: If a magazine or journal decides to publish an article you write, be sure to include your contact information (phone number, e-mail, snail mail, etc.) so that interested readers can contact you in the future.

Some people refer to these as "authority articles" because you are being published and thus, have some kind of authority. Published clips and articles add value to your promotional material; you suddenly become more acceptable, powerful and useful to others.

Here are some of those ways of getting in front of the right audience:

➡ Write articles for trade publications and offer them (initially) for free;

➡ Sponsor a breakfast networking meeting for people in your target industry or market;

➡ Create and mail a low-cost direct mail piece;

➡ Attend watering hole meetings;

➡ Create your own newsletter;

➡ Make more phone calls;

➡ Walk through more buildings, business and industrial parks and complexes, collecting business cards and dropping yours off;

➡ Make *more* phone calls; and

➡ Brainstorm with non-competing colleagues. You may need to go outside your office or industry, but that's okay.

Move the Sale Forward

The greater the variety of points of view you gather, the clearer it will be to you what you are comfortable with and how you can shape these ideas into a business plan for yourself.

The great thing about the three-point business plan is that it does not create conflict or put you at cross purposes with the business and marketing plan your company has in place. The company must worry about the overall game plan. You have to run with the ball and try to score. If the game plan is to beat the competition, your business plan will help you achieve that. If the game plan is to own more market share or ensure a higher profit margin or increase penetration into a territory, your business plan will help achieve that, as well.

Often sales management concepts and objectives sound militant or battle-oriented in nature. It's true that the competition is one of the key obstacles you must overcome in winning and keeping clients. It's also true that each new client brought in is like winning control of a strategic location. And most importantly, both military and sales campaigns require discipline, focus, knowledge of the terrain and a tremendous amount of personal commitment by each person on the front lines.

The front line people get a lot of the glory with good reason: They're the ones taking most of the risk. There's risk in looking for new business.

There's risk in going to networking meetings, where you may not know anyone. There's risk in writing something that may be refuted or challenged later. But sales is another word for risk. A recent ad campaign for a financial management company uses the line: *The greatest risk is not taking one*. Amen to that! Every useful and honorable endeavor begins with the belief that we can make a difference. If not in our own lives and careers, then in the lives of others.

> The tactics to implement in your plan appear throughout this book—the 20 Call Burst; open-ended questions; writing authoritative articles, etc. With tools and the tactics with which to pursue your chosen targets, time is the next point on the plan.

Time is your most available resource. You may feel as though you don't have time to get tasks finished to your satisfaction, but one thing that I have realized is that we have all the time we need. Time management is a great concept, but in real life, we cannot manage time. We can only manage what we do inside packets of time. From seven in the morning until noon, I choose to do _____. At seven in the evening until eleven, I choose to do _____.

When I use time as the third point of my business plan, I carve out time on my calendar to actually accomplish the things I say I want to do. If I am going to do a mailer to one thousand people, I must accomplish certain things in advance. This moves me to set a delivery date on my calendar. This then causes me to plan when the final copy and graphics must be done, in order to live up to that delivery date.

The promises you make to yourself are the easiest to break, which is why you must hold yourself accountable and not turn into a dispenser of excuses.

Time, being our third point, moves you to plan. You must commit to what you will do inside packets of time.

One thing you can count on if you come to my office on a day when I am not traveling, is that within 20 minutes of unlocking the door, I've begun a 20 Call Burst.

Again, plan what you will do inside packets of time. Take your planner out and look for the first day that has nothing planned right now. Yes—now! Add something that will help you initiate your tactics and get you in front of your targets. In all, you must attach a specific value to your time. For most, every minute of the day has value. You'll want to use every minute to move conversations—and ultimately yourself—forward.

Conclusion: Your Ideas and Your Account

Everything starts with an idea. Man going into space; the Declaration of Independence; even the pyramids began with an idea. At some point, someone had to write the idea down, share it with others and then act on it. It's important to keep track of your ideas, no matter how minuscule you think they are. The world is waiting for your ideas!

The three-point business plan is just that—a plan. Plans do not run themselves, nor do they challenge your creativity and execute themselves by sitting on paper in a drawer. Now that you have these tools to consider, people to target and tactics to implement, use time to make it all come to life in your selling career.

Cavett Robert, the founder of The National Speaker's Association, once said: "Every day, we are given 24 non-refundable fragments of eternity. Yesterday is a cancelled check, tomorrow is a promissory note— only *now* is negotiable."

Think about what that statement means: *non-refundable fragments of eternity*. The next time you feel like you don't have enough time, stop and think about what the most important thing you can do with the time you have is—because *now* is all you've got! It's important, each day, to think about:

- Who you care about;

- What you add to their lives;

- What you have in life that you appreciate *right now*; and

- What you get out of the effort you put into your daily labor.

Funny how earnings per share and hours logged at the office don't flash into your head when you really sit and think about your priorities. Twenty-four non-refundable fragments are deposited into your account every time you wake from sleep. How much is that worth to you?

Chapter 10:
Moving Management
Conversations Forward

Sales isn't always about direct contact with clients. If you're a good salesperson, you'll eventually be put in charge of other sales people. Interaction, supervision and leadership of subordinates are issues discussed in many books at great length. Our focus when discussing moving management conversations forward will be the sales manager-salesperson relationship.

Sales people are loathe to be managed, and for good reason. They tend to be fiercely independent and they don't like the constraints of a standard job. "Jobs" (according to sales people) are restrictive; jobs are for people with a different world view; and jobs are for people who possess a different sense of self than sales people.

Something in Common

I once sat in a sales meeting with a supervisor of mine when I worked in the employment agency business in Los Angeles. The supervisor was talking about how difficult it was to recruit new employees to the agency, which seemed ironic given the company was dedicated to matching people with jobs. She told our small group of unique people that we had some characteristics in common.

Move the Sale Forward

As soon as the words left her lips, three of us looked around the meeting, thinking the exact same thing. We each doubted, based on experience with each other so far, that we had anything in common. My supervisor continued:

You all like to read. You all think you know when something is really funny, or if it's stupid, and people who laugh at stupid humor just don't see how uninspired the humor is. You all have one close friend that you feel you can tell anything to, and you all feel as though you're not making the kind of money you think you should. Some of you think the shortfall in income is because of our "unfair" commission structure, but most of you think the reason for the shortfall is due to your not working hard enough. You're rarely satisfied with your own performance.

I was stupefied, wondering how she'd gotten this information about me. Over the water cooler later that day, two different people shared the same reaction with me. All that she said struck a cord with us because she was right in a lot of ways.

My supervisor had been in sales and the employment agency business for many years, and she had seen people come and go. She was not impressed with "flash in the pan" sales people, or those who arrive on the scene, close one large or several average-sized deals within weeks of being hired, then never produce another deal despite all the accolades. Many of these people leave the business, blaming others for their failure. My supervisor had outlived all of these types. She'd been dealing with her clients, closing her deals and building a bigger business long after the flash in the pan left.

She had become a supervisor as the result of her consistency and determination. She paid very close attention to the people with whom she helped place in jobs. She knew that if she didn't connect with her candidates, they wouldn't perform well on interviews and her reputation would suffer. By the same token, she had learned, and demonstrated to us, that long-term, productive relationships with the people reporting to her required the same skills. She and I talked about the fact that telling people what to do was not the best way to help them work independently. She also recognized, practiced and taught me how valuable the application of consistency could be to my personal selling career.

One way to maintain consistency is to keep things simple. If you deal with customers in the same way you deal with your spouse, you'll have a better chance of being genuine because you're not creating a different persona for different situations.

Moving management conversations forward means using the skills we have discussed so far, maintaining a consistent approach and thought process and modifying our open-ended questions.

The content, or text of the questions may change, but the overall goal is the same: To move things forward. If sales people view their work as something other than a "job," it follows, then, that they'll view their immediate superior as someone other than a supervisor or boss.

Sales people want leadership but they don't want to be told what to do. Sales people want coaching but they don't want to be told that they're doing anything wrong. Sales people want feedback but they don't want to call a customer who might be having a problem. Sales people want to build relationships but they don't want to be stuck dealing with the same issues over and over again.

Sales people want incentives for exceeding quota but they don't want to be treated like an also-ran if they fall short of quota.

Managing sales people is like walking up to a bee hive, smacking it with a stick and then working to get all of the bees that frantically fly out to fly in one direction at the exact same speed. When I was the general sales manager for Nationwide Cellular in Southern California, I held managers meetings every month.

> For readers who manage multiple locations with a management team, if it's financially and geographically feasible, bring your team of managers together a few times a year at the absolute least. It's amazing the difference with which people will approach and resolve the same problem in person versus over the phone. In addition, every one of your managers (and your sales people) has different skills, tricks and techniques. You probably have a huge storage of knowledge among your team that you have a greater ability to tap by having them in the same room than any other environment.

In my assigned region, seven managers reported to me. They all managed other locations, each with an average of five sales people. I brought these managers together once a month. We would talk, debate and work through as many issues as we could before lunch. I used to affectionately refer to these meetings as wrestling matches because of the high level of determination and energy required to keep these dynamic, intelligent people on topic—for a long time—in order to reach some decisions. I absolutely loved these meetings, but was mentally exhausted when they were over.

I learned in these meetings that sales management had to be about connecting with the people, managing my expectations, hearing people out and not forgetting what it was that they told me.

Sales management is synonymous with multiple process management in that the sales manager cannot (and should not) try to manage each step of the process for sales people, but rather find a way to have a level of involvement that keeps multiple activities moving forward.

There are issues to stay on top of, ranging from what your direct reports are doing and what the current inventory is, to what activities the sales people are putting a high priority on (and this will not always coincide with what you make a priority).

You must maintain the balance between generating revenue and generating profit. If you sell a higher dollar amount in sales than you did last quarter, it must follow that the profit margin has been maintained, before you can declare a solid increase.

When you move management conversations forward you need to keep track of what people say on multiple fronts. Managing sales people (or sales managers) requires that you:

- Understand the market they sell in;

- Have an appreciation for the competitive challenges in that market;

- Leave people room to make some errors, and allow them to find, assess and repair those errors;

- Be able to distinguish between a reason for sales not to increase and an excuse;

- Realize that people will show you things about themselves because they choose to, not because they think your finding out will be a revelation to you; and

- Have a sense of humor.

Sales people like to laugh. They like to laugh at themselves and the ridiculous things that happen in their profession. Every profession has its hard-to-believe stories and sales is no exception. My simple philosophy for those folks that have a hard time bringing their sense of humor to work is this: If it's not fun, stop doing it!

As a manager, it's essential to understand the market that a salesperson sells into. You have to keep your eyes on:

Move the Sale Forward

- Who the salesperson tends to bring in and maintain as customers; and

- The people that are in the pipeline and who may be potential customers in the future.

Qualifying your sales people's targets is important because you want both the prospective customer and the salesperson to maintain expectations you can either meet or exceed as a vendor.

 Remember: To qualify = to meet specific criteria.

Having an appreciation for the competitive challenges reduces conversations focused on minor issues, like the difference in price between what you offer and what the competition has sold in the past. Sales people are, at times, more effective negotiators with people inside their company than outside. They have a protectionist attitude toward their client base, and want to make and keep their clients happy.

What sometimes happens, though, is that sales people make one of two common mistakes. These mistakes are often made with the right intentions, but a mistake is a mistake, regardless of intent. These two common mistakes are:

1) They begin to believe that what the customer wants (or what they think the customer needs) is more important than rate, price and policy integrity; and

2) They begin to believe that their customers are theirs and not the company's.

This may sound controversial to some sales people reading this, but stay with me. If you are an employee (or independent contractor) whose agreement with a company has that company paying for support, technology, health insurance, payroll, phones, office space and more, then the customers you bring in are customers of the company.

I am not so naïve as to think that should one of my sales people eventually move on, he or she won't attempt to continue a relationship with those prospects and customers. This entire book is about the human connection and how people tend to buy from people they are comfortable with. But the bottom line is that your employer shoulders the greater percentage of risk in most salesperson/employer relationships, and lowering the expectation bar over and over again to accommodate someone (as the salesperson) or the customer does no one any good. Profit is the main reason companies exist. That profit is compromised when we lose sight of our non-negotiable standards at any level. Sales people who are elevated into management (as I was) have a difficult time making the transition in how one must look at these types of issues.

This is why moving management conversations forward is mentioned here.

Setting Standards

As a salesperson, I am very focused on moving all conversations forward as quickly as I can. When I hit a roadblock (whether real or perceived) disguised as an objection (or management not wanting to bend for a client) I have been known to allow my emotions to get the better of me.

There were plenty of times when I was in the placement/employment industry when I was asked by a prospect to "give them some room" on our agreed-upon fee. Translation: "I want a discount." As a salesperson, when I hear this, my heart rate goes up for a few different reasons.

Move the Sale Forward

1) I feel as though I am close to a deal, and that is exciting!;

2) I fear that if I do not agree, all the work I have done up to this point will be lost without acquiring a commission;

3) If I bend now, I will be setting a precedent; and

4) I will lose the prospect's respect.

Notice how much fear and loss show up in the previous potential scenarios. All of these are based on experience, and they do not just go away. I raise this issue here because as sales managers, we must set non-negotiable standards with our staff as well as customers. If one of your sales people is on the phone with a prospect and the prospect says: "Let me talk to your boss," because they want to deal with a higher authority, as manager you have a judgment call to make should you accept the call.

If you bend because you need the revenue to achieve the goal you have ultimate responsibility for, you must think about what that tells your staff. If you bend because that company can possibly bring a ton of revenue to you and your salesperson in the future, you must think about what that tells your staff.

On the other hand, if you do not bend, you probably will not be asked to handle these types of calls too many more times. How you manage and what standards you set, are up to you. I, personally, did not want to have to be the final authority for my sales people because then their role becomes diminished in the eyes of the buyer. The buyer tended to ask for me more than his assigned salesperson, and that is not the succession of events I wanted to create.

> Sales people will be as interested in holding you, their manager, accountable for changing standards as you hold them accountable for activity levels.

Chapter 10: Moving Management Conversations Forward

They will look to you for leadership, guidance and ideas. The onus on you as a manager, then, is to be in touch with what techniques each of your people adopt, apply and believe in.

Sales people don't want to hear suggestions from their managers that they've already tried and that didn't work. Sales people are like anyone else when it comes to their perception of the amount of attention you as a sales manager give them. If the attention you pay someone is due to a shortfall in the salesperson's results, the simplest description (and the general perception) of this is bad attention.

If attention is paid because a salesperson is doing well, and you as a manager are offering accolades, support or encouragement, then this is perceived as good attention.

> **Managing sales people means performing a balancing act between keeping them focused and productive and making sure they don't get too full of themselves.**

Successful sales managers help their sales people build skills and confidence, which generates results in turn. It can get tricky, however, managing sales people once they become top performers. The person who you've helped become a powerful force in your company and a recognized name with your customers now thinks he/she is entitled to an endless supply of perks and kudos. This is where moving sales management conversations forward comes into play.

Sales people who bring in large transactions, representing high dollars, may lean on that accomplishment as a replacement to building new business. Large transactions represent large customers or revenue streams. The person between you as a manager and that customer is your salesperson.

Instead of generating 20 Call Bursts and bringing in new accounts, these sales people regularly talk about how much time their monster account requires of them.

There's a solution to dealing with this, and it has to do with the three levels of performance.

Three Levels Of Performance

Most sales teams can be divided into three groups. Each group is characterized by what contribution each person in the group makes. Sales will always be about results. The percentage of contribution each person makes, measured in dollars and cents, determines which group they are categorized into. Let's quickly describe each of these groups.

The first, or top level, comprises the top performers—people who are reliably over quota. They need close attention from their managers and deserve it. Sales managers have quotas, which are achieved via the sales their sales people produce. As a manager of sales people, you'll want to have a clear, positive channel of communication with those who are responsible for the larger portion of the quota.

Items on a sales manager's compensation package may include targets and rewards attached to:

- Override;

- Percent of attainment *of* quota; and

- Percent of attainment *above* quota.

We must remind and assist top performers to maintain a stream of prospective new business. If more than 15 percent of any revenue segment comes from one customer, then you and the salesperson are at risk.

Chapter 10: Moving Management Conversations Forward

The risk lies in the potential for damage to your production, should that customer go away.

With markets changing, people moving and competition nipping at your heels, top performers must not and cannot rest on their laurels. Your time with them should include a discussion about development of new business throughout their selling year.

Each of these represents a benchmark that sales managers use to compute their income. Don't forget about the 80/20 principle here: Eighty percent of the quota for a region or group is usually assigned to and attained by 20 percent of the sales force.

The second—middle group—is made up of people who are either on their way to becoming a part of the top group or are intermittently "at" or "just below" quota. These are great people to have on the team; they are the bread and butter of the sales managers' production responsibility.

These folks understand (and, thankfully, practice) consistency, and they reliably produce. Sometime they feel entitled to as much attention as they see the heavy-hitting top performers receiving, and with good reason. We are constantly watching to be sure these folks continue to produce, rather than falter toward becoming part of the lower third.

The lower third is another group that deserves a lot of attention, but these sales people don't necessarily want the kind of attention they're going to get from their manager. There are a multitude of factors as to why someone's production may be down. Although they will resist any attention you give them because they will think that it only points to their inadequacy, it's key to keep close watch on their activity, motivation level, desire to work and understanding of the importance of their turning things around.

If you are not performing, you know it, your peers know it…and your manager knows it.

This lower third is comprised of people moving in one of two directions: On their way up to the middle third or on their way out of the company. Some refer to the people in this position as "on the bubble," because if performance doesn't increase, the proverbial bubble will burst and they'll find themselves in a position to pursue opportunities elsewhere. In other words, they'll be fired.

Attention must be paid to these people. An investment of time must be made because sales and sales people are constantly in flux. Conditions, moods, levels of confidence and relationships change. The sales manger must find a way to stay in step with as much of this as possible. Knowing when you need to fire someone can be tough. If, after a reasonable amount of training, time and patience, you still have sales people under you who don't produce, you need to think about firing them. It's for their own good, the good of their peers and the good of the customer base they are calling on.

Keeping It Simple

Managing people is hard to do. No matter your intelligence, educational or experience level, working and dealing with people is challenging. How often, for example, do you find it hard to figure out the perfect thing to say to someone you're trying to manage? Probably fairly often. The decisions you make when working to increase a salesperson's overall performance are important—and unfortunately, it's not immediately apparent if we have made the right or wrong decision. It's key to learn and master the skills related to how to conduct exit interviews, disciplinary actions, skill development conversations and policy and procedure corrections in a decent, effective way. The best way to approach all of these things is to keep it simple and direct.

> **Managing sales people means working to keep a raging fire from consuming a portion of the forest, while still making sure that the fire never goes out.**

Chapter 10: Moving Management Conversations Forward

Earlier I mentioned how there's a danger in developing someone into a top sales performer. Top performers can quickly see themselves as bulletproof and needing less direction, development and management feedback. As a sales manager, you need to pay even closer attention to these top performers. You must continue to manage them in the sense that you funnel, direct and sharpen their energy. We all need mentors and leadership. We all need someone to be unbiased about our performance, skills and level of output. Sales managers fill this special role, becoming guiding lights from the low-end newbie to the top salesperson of the month. By keeping it simple, I am referring to a few concepts:

- The conversations we have with sales people must be focused on behaviors and results, as opposed to past events or emotions. (We mentioned in Chapter 2 that the best way to direct a conversation is to keep emotion out of it.);

- We must ask simple, direct questions confined to issues that will help the salesperson win more business; and

- The conversations between you and your sales people should result in both of you feeling as though you are both moving forward, together!

15 Minutes of Fame

One tool I used as a corporate sales manager was a one-page document I called "15 minutes of fame." I allowed my sales people 15 minutes to update me on their progress and future goals. On the next page is a sample copy of what I'd have my sales people fill out:

Move the Sale Forward

15 Minutes of Fame

1) **Targets**
    a) _____
    b) _____
    c) _____
    d) _____
    e) _____
    f) _____

2) **Tactics**
    a) _____
    b) _____
    c) _____
    d) _____

3) **Hot Deals**
    a) _____
    b) _____
    c) _____
    d) _____
    e) _____

4) **Last Week's Accomplishments:**
    a) _____
    b) _____
    c) _____
    d) _____

5) **This Week's Goals:**
    a) _____
    b) _____
    c) _____
    d) _____
    e) _____

Chapter 10: Moving Management Conversations Forward

Best thing about this week:

_____

_____

_____

_____

Every Friday, I'd make appointments for individual meetings with sales reps. The appointments would be for a 15-minute meeting the following week, preferably on a Monday or Tuesday. These meetings would unfold according to a multi-step agenda. In these meetings, the reps would:

1) Share with me their percent of attainment of the previous week's sales goal;

2) Tell me what prospects they considered to be hot (high potential to close) and the projected time frame to close (or lose) the deal;

3) Tell me what their goal was for the current selling week; and

4) Tell me something good that happened the previous week, which they felt would impact their business, approach, competitive stance or personal commitment to staying motivated.

The goal was to have them end the meeting with a combination of something positive to talk about, and for them to realize that their being motivated was mostly their responsibility. It took time for my reps to get used to this weekly lesson. It had a huge impact on how we communicated, how comfortable I was with how they spent their time…and guess what? Our sales increased! They were now required to prepare a document and a presentation for me, every week.

They'd get a chance to compare earlier documents with the current one in order to track their progress regarding conversations they were having with prospects, customers, leads and referral sources. It also opened up their eyes to holes in their selling techniques. They were able to pinpoint lost clients and big deals that hadn't materialized and evaluate how they spent their time. When someone comes to me with his 15 minutes of fame form, it's his opportunity to wow me.

> **By committing to and living up to a regular, scheduled time to track activity, renew focus and measure results, folks started coming to me sooner with problems, allowing us to prepare for—and even solve those problems—before they got out of hand.**

In addition, the tenor of our conversations soon took on the mood and focus I wanted them to. At first, as with all change, there was resistance and skepticism about the reasons for what we were doing. There was even, to a certain extent, suspicion that the exercise was designed to get people in trouble. Far from it.

Some even thought 15 minutes of fame was going to strictly be a disciplinary tool. Wrong again.

People either warmed to the idea, and we increased their sales, my overall production and everyone's income, or they resisted, lost track of what they were doing, failed to accurately report how in control of their business they were and eventually left on their own.

Most sales environments are very open with information. The person who is number one in sales for the month, year, quarter or even the day is rarely a secret.

Everyone knows who is number one and who is in last place.

When folks had a problem with 15 minutes of fame, it was because they had little to feel famous about.

Open-Ended Killer Questions For Managers

We must be able to inquire about the status of deals, databases, expensed activities and anything else that impacts the bottom line with which a salesperson ends each measured period.

This opens the door for us to establish some open-ended killer questions that managers will find useful.

Asking "Did you close that deal yet?" is closed-ended…and won't get you the kind of information you really want. Asking: "Where are you as far as the ABC deal?" may get you a broad answer because there is a wide range of information the a salesperson can share regarding the status.

Instead, you should focus your questions in the same manner as all open-ended questions: on the person, and how he thinks, feels and perceives things, as opposed to nailing him to the wall for a "yes" or "no" answer. To that end, some examples of good questions include:

- "What can I do to help you prepare for 15 minutes of fame?"

- "How comfortable are you with making the top of the performance list this month?"

- "Where are you in the process of the deals we discussed last week?"

- "What needs to happen before you can plug cold calling back into your plan?"

- "What do you need from me in order to increase your effectiveness over the next few months?"

- "What's the latest?"

- "What can I do to get some obstacles out of your way?"

- "What's the best thing that's happened in the last few days?"

Take a minute or two to think about some questions that will get your sales people talking to you, instead of reporting to you. Ask questions that are designed to help you learn something, instead of putting them on the spot. Ask some friends to listen to these and see how they would react if their supervisor asked them similar questions. As with open-ended killer questions discussed earlier in this book, it takes thought, practice and practical application to begin to develop this skill, as well as a large commitment of time and effort to master it.

The focus of these questions must be on your sales people, and not their behaviors, in order to create the dialogue that will give you the information you want and allow them to talk to you about their business. I always refer to a salesperson's area of responsibility as "their business" as opposed to "their job."

Best and Worst

When I ran a team of about eight people, I liked to spring the best/worst story on them about two or three times a month. Best/worst was a quick exercise where I would allow them to get a horror story off their chest or talk about some activity or meeting that went particularly well for them that week.

The group—not me—chose whose story was best or worst. This way, it was an exercise I suggested and led, instead of managed. The ground rules are simple. Your story must:

- Be true;

- Be about you, not someone you know;

- Have happened since the last meeting; and

- Be able to be expressed in less than five minutes.

The setup was simple: I closed out all of the final business of the meeting and said: "Okay, who had something really good or really bad happen since we were together last?"

A few people would tell their stories, and we would either sympathize, laugh or applaud. The person with the best story got a free lunch from me that day. The person with the worst experience would receive a small cash bonus for sticking with the profession…and telling the story.

The benefit of hearing the good story is obvious: it gave us all hope or something to laugh about before beginning the selling day. The bad experience was just as valuable because it gave us all a sense that whatever happens—no matter how bad—we know that a good story is probably right around the corner.

Conclusion

Moving sales management conversations forward is a challenge, a thrill and a burden. It requires the best we have to offer. It requires selflessness with the goal of achieving something exciting and worthwhile through—and with—other people. It may not be for everyone, but the folks that do take on the challenge are to be commended and respected.

In the next chapter, we discuss the three essential life skills. These will be the things you must master not only as a salesperson, but as a human being trying to succeed in this competitive world.

Move the Sale Forward

Chapter 11:
Sales Skills...and
Life Skills

In order for us to survive in life, there are a few essential skills we need to master, which no one ever teaches us. These skills not only give us an advantage, they also help us establish a sense of flow and order in our lives—forward motion. You might wonder why we go into detail here about finding work, which is one of the essential skills, but it's as key to being successful in sales as the other two essential skills—maintaining relationships and communicating. And, if you can master all three life skills, you'll find professional selling all the more rewarding.

In the truest form of the word, a *skill* is a process or activity, which can be learned. With this as the good news, let's look at each skill, what it takes to master each skill and how they interrelate.

Essential Life Skill 1: How to Find Work

At the turn of the Twentieth Century, Henry Ford introduced the 40-hour work week. This is one of the many ways his ideas reshaped today's world. First, he decided that since it took a variety of small, menial tasks, done in a specific order, to complete the larger task of creating a completed automobile, people would need to be focused on regularly performing those small, menial tasks. He wanted them to perform those tasks over and over, and be a part of a larger group. He wanted them to see cars leaving the factory at the end of the week. He wanted them to have a sense of participation in the broader picture, and more importantly, his goal was to make it possible for those people to be able to afford to buy one of the products they helped create.

By introducing the standard work week and payroll system, Ford made an immeasurable impact on the working world. But fast forward to the Twenty-first Century and our lives today. We've grown accustomed to the standard work week…but something else has changed. We no longer work for the same company our entire lives. The idea of someone graduating from school, staying at a company for 20 or 30 years and then retiring with a gold watch is almost comical.

Friends and colleagues of mine have held multiple positions with a variety of companies. The old stigma of perceiving someone who has changed jobs as a "job hopper" has virtually disappeared. We can no longer look at the time and effort we spend each work day as a "job."

So, even though the 40-hour work week remains, the definition of "career" and "job" has shifted. We now must be able to find "work" as opposed to simply a job.

A *job* is something that requires specific skills or abilities, which are clearly defined. The job, in its most basic sense, is a regular repetition of individual tasks. The job provides limited opportunity with which to grow personally (or professionally) and contribute to an outcome or product. Jobs offer safety, security and protection.

Work, on the other hand, demands more of us. Viewing what we do to earn money and provide for ourselves (and our family) as work instead of a job, allows us to view it as something that may not be easily classified and defined. This leads to the fact that we may offer more than what can be put into a job description. The reason I go into this level of detail is that finding a job is not an essential life skill. Most people can fall into jobs, get referred into jobs, or land a job because the place of employment happens to be hiring.

Finding work means you view who you are, what you offer and how you fit into the greater employment landscape as someone more unique, more valuable and—most importantly—more in control of your ability to generate an income.

When I talk to people looking for work, my first question is: "What do you really want to do?" For the people who say they want to be involved in a creative endeavor (i.e., an actor, musician, artist), the next thing out of their mouth usually is: "But I'm not sure I could afford to do that."

What this says to me is that a lifestyle or income level has a higher priority to them than actually doing what they feel passionate about for a living. There are far too many people in this world who walk through their lives doing "jobs" as opposed to being involved in the profession they feel they were born to work in. So, the question we are addressing is: "How do we find work?"

> **The difference between "finding work" and "getting a job" is as fine a distinction as that between trying to close someone today and moving the conversation forward toward a sale.**

Finding work means that we want to make some sort of bottom line contribution, whether it's for our employer or our own business. There is an entrepreneurial mindset required for this search process because we take responsibility for generating revenue and agree to have what we contribute measured in dollars and sense.

Finding work means we follow the guidelines outlined throughout this book for selling a product or service. Of all the products and services one can sell, the most important is selling yourself to an employer. Lack of knowledge is no sin. It does, however, deprive us of certain opportunities and entrees.

In order for us to sell ourselves, we must identify what it is that we can bring to the table, which has specific, identifiable value. We must be able to define our service.

Why? Because today the impact you make as a member of a company determines whether or not you continue to work.

We immediately put ourselves at a disadvantage, because we don't know the ins and outs of the interviewing, search and selection process.

I learned much of what we'll discuss in the rest of this section by working as a recruiter. There are subtle reasons (that are almost considered trade secrets) why some people acquire prime positions in companies and receive offers and others don't. No one is keeping this information from the public; it's just that most people don't take the time to investigate these issues.

Selling Yourself

Let's use Alice as an example. Alice finds herself unemployed after being laid off. Because the decision as to whether or not she finds employment again is in someone else's hands, she feels she is on the weak side of the negotiation. As soon as she believes that, she's correct…and in trouble.

Prior to losing her job, Alice analyzed economic data and translated it into profit potential projections. Her numbers and translation helped her employer set pricing that was not based on cost of production plus cost of sale. She helped her employer have a sense of what the market will bear.

Very sophisticated stuff, right? But when Alice's former employer was purchased by Conglomo Enterprises, she no longer had the position. She was suddenly on the outside, looking in, wondering what happened. The new, larger owner is still using her economic models to set pricing, and three months later, they report their highest sales quarter ever!

She should use this information as fuel for her work search but, since Alice feels as though she's at a disadvantage, her creativity is blocked. She's looking through the classifieds, searching for an ad that includes: "Must be able to create and employ sophisticated economic models to help company set prices."

She's probably not going to find that ad.

So, what's the solution?

Alice needs to take a look at a new set of skills that will prevent this experience from happening again. She cannot control what Conglomo Enterprises does and she cannot prevent the next company she works for from, downsizing, rightsizing or going out of business.

The fact is that the marketplace, while a vicious, competitive world, is not required to provide Alice a living. It's not required to make sure that people have jobs that are secure or that their bosses are nice to them. The marketplace is designed to, and fully expects to, make a profit. Alice needs to learn and master the first essential life skill: *how to find work.*

Alice's first step is to create a statement that she can deliver confidently and quickly, which will give the person with whom she is speaking a clear idea of her skills and abilities. It's not easy.

Begin with a Definition of Service

If someone met you on an elevator at a convention and asked you what you did for a living, how would you respond? Use the space below to answer that question, in writing:

1)   **What do you *Do*?**

_____

_____

_____

Move the Sale Forward

Boil down your answer to one or two quick sentences, which will make the inquirer ask more questions. Your answers may lead to a longer conversation. This is where our friend Alice must begin.

In order to create her definition of service, she must take an inventory of:

- What she knows;

- What she can do;

- What her experience is;

- What she likes to do;

- What she does not like to do;

- How far she's willing to commute;

- What her "bottom economic line" is;

- How challenged she wants to be;

- How important "fun" is to her;

- How to help people understand (and want to learn more) about what she does;

- What the total value of all of her attributes are;

- What sort of work environment allows her to be most productive;

- How much money she wants to make; and

- What things she's willing to trade off or do without to make the money she wants.

After carefully detailing her responses on paper, she must prioritize them as objectively as possible.

Alice's knowledge is going to be extremely useful to her next employer. What she does with that knowledge and how she applies it to help her new company make money is more important. The line between knowledge and wisdom is as fuzzy as the one between experience and application of that experience. When we're selling our self (looking for work), we're selling an intangible thing. Résumés are tangible things to show what someone has done in the past...but they can't prove that the person actually possesses the listed skills and qualities.

When you sell yourself through a résumé, you're hoping to get an invite to an interview. A résumé's goal is strictly to have the person reading it want to find out more. Since we're conditioned to view the work search as one where the employer is the one who'll provide us with a job, we feel as though we're at a disadvantage. Looking for work is not playing the lottery. It's not all up to chance.

It's a romantic dance of negotiation and creativity. Remember: The person who gets the best "job" is not always the most qualified. It's the person who has sold himself better than any other candidate.

At the outset of the search, and during the initial interviews, it's difficult for us to feel as though we're in a strong negotiating position, mostly because we view the employer as the person in control. In my experience as a recruiter and executive employment coach, it usually comes as a revelation to people that the point of an interview (from the potential employee's point of view) is strictly to get to the next step—to, in effect, move the conversation forward.

I spend a fair amount of time dissuading people from going to an interview "to see if they will like the job." They cannot get a realistic view of a job and what it's like to work for a company from the first interview. Each party is sizing the other up, to see if they like each other.

When Alice goes on her first interview with Conglomo Enterprises' competitor, she should keep in mind that her interviewer is not trying to figure out if Alice knows everything about the job, or determine her ability to outperform what she accomplished with Conglomo.

Move the Sale Forward

The interviewer is trying to get a sense of whether or not she will fit in at the company. Alice must be careful not to focus on the requirements, hours, overtime or view out of her office window during the first interview. Her assignment is to get to the second interview. That's all.

She must, then, employ the first step for selling professionally: imagination. She needs to imagine her employer (or client) enjoying the benefits of what she offers. Since she knows that people buy based on emotion, and that hiring someone is more often than not an issue of chemistry over documented experience, she knows that her job is to move the conversation forward.

> The reason we must not go into interviews trying to decide if we want the job or not, is that we can never have an objective perspective while trying to hold the attention of (and pay attention to) the interviewer.

Interviewing is a very demanding mental and emotional exercise. We tend to try to think about too much during interviews, and increase our potential for getting distracted. If I engage in an interview with you, and while you are talking, you're thinking more about whether or not you like the color of paint on the walls than you are about what I'm saying, we both lose.

I recommend the following: Every interview you go on, do what you can to show enthusiasm for the position and the prospect of going to work there. If you walk out without an offer, then you feel at a disadvantage. If you walk out *with* an offer, then you are in complete control over whether you go to work there or not. There will be ample time after the interview to evaluate the pros and cons. You have much more of an objective view of whether or not you want to work for a company when you don't feel the pressure to make an immediate decision or don't create that kind of pressure on the spot.

The appropriate time to decide whether or not to accept employment is: after it has been offered to you and not before. In another sense, the appropriate time to celebrate a sale is after the commission check clears your bank.

This puts you in a position of power. If someone offers you employment, it means he/she wants you. If you don't want this particular offer, you are in complete control and have broken no rules by turning the offer down. Many people, once they turn down an offer, feel exhilarated. They mentally review all the things they learned in the third or fourth interview that did not (and will never) come out in the first interview. Interacting with people is the best way to get a sense of a company's work environment, ethics, level of professionalism, etc.

When you're on your third interview and walk around the company, try to find a reason to go into the company break room, kitchen or lunch room. The people milling around in there won't know who you are or why you are there. They will assume you belong there and will almost never give you a second thought. Get a drink of water or buy a soda out of the vending machine. The tone (and content) of conversations in that environment will give you a sense of the mood of the place.

If people are talking animatedly about a recent company event or a client or project, this can indicate that they are enjoying themselves. If their expressions are dour and they don't appear to be excited about being there, you have a different picture.

Back to Alice's definition of *service*. On the first and every subsequent interview, she must be clear and confident in expressing her definition of service. A definition of service statement is similar to what we outlined in a previous chapter, where we discussed the components of a strong identification statement as part of your strong opening. Before you ask that first open-ended killer question, you must identify yourself, your company and then state your purpose for the call.

Move the Sale Forward

This means that when you introduce yourself, you must have your definition of service statement ready. It should indicate something fairly jazzy about what you do. You want it to have a bit of sizzle. The goal is to have the other person want you to explain it in more detail.

> This is a great place to incorporate emotional trigger words. What has Alice done in the past that would be of interest or have value for a potential employer? Not tasks. Results: "In my previous position with Conglomo, I made money for the company."

Keep in mind that we must not presuppose how what we do is going to benefit a potential employer. We must keep our definition of service statement general enough so that when a question is asked, we can steer the conversation toward the other person's business, problem or concern. Once we do that and get them talking, we can ask our own questions based on what they have said. We then move the sale forward.

Try your definition of service statement out on friends and business associates. Most people have, at some time in their life, been unemployed and looking for a job, so most can relate. As a result, people's empathy and willingness to offer suggestions might surprise you!

When we tell people we are unemployed, it makes us feel bad—uncomfortable—because we feel as though our value as a person has diminished. This is a cultural issue and there is not much you can do about it. What you can do, however, is go to people you trust, tell them you are looking for work and that you have a unique approach to selling yourself you want to test out on them. You won't be counting on your friends for job leads, but they are a good source of encouragement and feedback. This makes it easier to develop a plan, modify it and execute it.

> Mailing out 50 résumés on Monday and counting zero interviews on Friday is not something that we use as a reliable measurement item. Mailing out 50 résumés on Monday and generating two 20 Call Bursts before Friday, on the other hand, is a reliable measurement. Being diligent and realistic is important in our work search.

By defining her service, Alice now can converse with people on a different level. They'll ask her how she got into that specific type of work. They'll ask if she really likes it. Employers are looking for potential employees who'll be happy providing the service that they outline in their résumé and interview.

One of my basic life philosophies is: *Find, pursue and learn about your chosen profession. Choose one that you feel will keep your interest, challenge your mind and fuel your passion.*

I've had many jobs in my life. When I finally found the work I wanted to do, I was a changed man.

I thoroughly enjoy the work I do. It took time to find it and even more time to become good at it. In my mind (and according to those closest to me), I became successful when I felt I needed to improve constantly. I enjoyed myself and was committed and energetic about it. I stopped counting the hours I was in the office. The clock almost became my enemy because I was more interested in getting more things done, than I was in finding out how long it would be until I could leave.

Alice's first interview now has a different objective. With a clearer objective and a positive approach she'll have more constructive results.

Finding work for Alice now means something totally different than "getting a job." She can operate from a position of greater confidence and take a macro view of both the process and her expected outcomes.

Move the Sale Forward

Now that her service has become defined, she must draw on another one of our elements to selling professionally: organization.

She must answer the question: "Who do I call?"

In answering the question *Who?*, Alice must first define a geographical boundary. When she decides how far she is willing to commute, it makes the chore of selecting target companies much easier. Too often we talk ourselves into tolerating a longer commute for a "great job." People go down that road with the best intentions and a few months into working at that great job, find themselves sorry they didn't maintain a non-negotiable geographical standard.

Alice must, at this point, acquire a map and draw a circle representing her ideal commute. If she's willing to relocate, her approach to the job hunt is more complicated, but it can still be managed and systematically attacked.

The next step is to define every company in a preferred geographical area that might ever have a need or use for Alice's service. Alice needs to be open to investigating companies that may not be in the exact industry she's used to working in. She must cast a wider net and be open to bringing in some fish she might not expect. This is the best time in her life to truly consider what she really wants to do.

Alice must not limit herself to those companies that are in direct competition with her former employer. She must also make sure, during the interview, not to bad-mouth her former employer or any other competition.

It doesn't matter if someone lacks personality or is unethical, and those facts are common knowledge in this industry. She must set some criteria for those she will approach to ensure that they are qualified. Once she defines her prospects, she must employ the hardest requirement for professional selling to apply when searching for work: discipline. When you don't have work, your job is to find work.

Now that Alice has all day to herself, she must set up a defined workspace in her home and set office hours. These office hours are not to be interrupted by playing with the cat, watching that great old movie she keeps missing or driving around aimlessly.

Sales people can think of a million reasons why a sale should not happen. People looking for work are convinced that there are a billion reasons why they won't find work.

Alice must focus on the fact that someone who has not learned of her unique combination of personality and experience, can now benefit by her being available. Alice can help someone's business grow. This won't happen, of course, until she sets some specific directed activity goals, gets the job and shows up at work every day.

Alice must get in the habit of making 20 Call Bursts every day to contact, introduce herself to and move conversations forward with prospective employers. Alice must move these conversations forward by asking open-ended killer questions that focus on the other person, and she must bring the conversation to the point where a face-to-face meeting is the interviewer's idea, and not hers.

Practical Application

When my friend Phil resigned from his position, he said it was "time for a change." He had worked in his chosen profession for some time and had tried a variety of formats and formulas to create the work environment nirvana he so passionately desired.

Move the Sale Forward

All of us talk about how we would change things if we could—and Phil had the chance to really reflect and evaluate his position, his worth and his interests.

Phil faced the same things as our fictional Alice. As of the first Monday following his departure from his former employer, Phil started working a specific plan. He made 20 Call Bursts in a specific geographical area, looking for people to invite him in for an interview, instead of responding to the Want Ads. He defined his service and marketed it to companies. Some of these companies were in the exact same business as his former employer.

Two and a half weeks into the process, he closed in on three separate offers of employment and was in a powerful position to choose his next step. He felt confident and relaxed. He had a sense of control and security.

Eventually, one of the companies he was interviewing with called him and asked: "If we were to make an offer to you at X income level, would you take it?" He called me and I told him to call them back and thank them for their time, but tell them that this not how you are accustomed to doing business and you'll probably be looking at other opportunities.

Like a good student, Phil called the potential employer and did just that. He made it clear that verbal—hypothetical—offers were not taken seriously for consideration. He wanted to thank them for considering him, but he would be looking elsewhere.

Within an hour, the person who originally interviewed him called him back, apologized for the mix-up and asked if he would still consider their offer if they could get a document in his hands the following day, via overnight delivery. Both Phil and I were impressed that when he turned the verbal offer down, they wanted to send a document with an offer outlined in specific detail. Maybe they thought he was a better negotiator than they realized—certainly a valuable skill to a sales-oriented organization!

> Employers are decision makers. They wake up every day looking for a good idea or a source of good ideas. They also want to know that regardless of the distractions, an employee will be able to execute the key activities and skills necessary to operate efficiently and effectively.

Phil was talented, knowledgeable and experienced. But when he began his search, he was feeling as though his stance in the marketplace was diminished because he was not gainfully employed. By working his plan and staying disciplined, he went out looking for work and it found him.

Our need to work, our drive to perform at work and the world's expectation that we work are inescapable issues. But somewhere over time and woven into our development, "work" changed to "job." A job is something society told us we must have in order to contribute. "Job" changed to "burden." Work needs to make a resurgence in our consciousness.

People who look for *work* as opposed to a *job* have an opportunity to make a difference, have fun and earn more. Those of us who view the work we do (and the service we provide) as work immediately change the perspective we operate under when interviewing. Protection and security are certainly benefits we would like to enjoy, but they are not the driving forces behind our search for work.

Refer to Appendix D for a worksheet you can use for when you need to commence a successful job search.

Essential Life Skill 2: Maintaining Relationships

Maintaining relationships is a slippery subject to tackle because men and women in general have different ideas of what a relationship is and what makes one work. Television and film comedies have made a fortune parodying and portraying the foibles of relationships. Some healthy, some not.

Our discussion of maintaining relationships assumes that relationships have some sort of life. They have an almost tangible aspect to them that we look for, try to sense and then react or respond to. We react or respond to the other person, not only based on what we want out of the relationship, but also upon our level of interest in maintaining the relationship.

When a relationship is meaningful (or potentially meaningful) to us, we are willing to make certain sacrifices to prevent losing that relationship and to have it move forward.

My most relevant experience is based on the sales and customer relationships I've maintained over time. I've learned the most from relationships that I was not successful at maintaining. I learned about appropriate and inappropriate questions. I learned about timing of conversations and pace of movement. I learned about the helplessness of loss.

Maintaining relationships is a skill-based activity that brings together much of what we've discussed so far.

> **The most powerful tool I have found in maintaining relationships has been humility.**

I may feel as though I know, and have command of, a variety of topics. But the relationship experience I have is probably similar to yours. We try to connect with someone, they hurt us or we hurt them, we apologize, try to recover and then move on. We move on, either with or without them, depending on the severity of the injury.

I know that maintaining relationships takes skill and it's so deeply and dramatically intertwined with the next skill we will discuss—how to communicate—that it's hard to distinguish the two.

Communication—the positive, progressive, exchange of ideas—is about listening and responding.

Maintaining relationships requires referencing or referring to the emotional tour we take with the other person. It requires that we chronicle or document what goes on and what the people involved agree to. Maintaining a sales relationship requires admitting mistakes (humility), listening more than talking (80/20 principle), documenting conversations (moving conversations forward) and paying attention to the human connections you make.

The skill of maintaining relationships is combining humility with the ability to overlook perceived injury. Though we live in a competitive world, and you may want all the business your current competitor has, you don't wish them any ill will. If you work hard and stay focused, you'll earn the business you deserve.

You need to view the business relationships you have as living, breathing entities—the survival of which depend on care, attention, patience and time.

Admission of Guilt

One of the least discussed, most often overlooked actions regarding maintaining any type of relationship is the willingness to admit when you've done something wrong. It's difficult to admit your errors regarding how you deal with people.

Move the Sale Forward

When you work out most of the emotional tension by talking to your friends, and you actually approach the person with whom you've acted inappropriately, you are taking a huge step in the right direction. The human connection sets you apart. It draws your relationships forward. It makes you feel as though you are a part of something.

As a salesperson, admitting that a promised delivery date will probably not be accurate is uncomfortable, but not the end of the world. What happens, however, is that we come across clients that, for whatever reason, we find it hard to admit errors to. We can be intimidated, we can be nervous that one mistake will cause the account to go away (or that our manager will take it away).

But when I have found the combination of humility and courage to approach someone with whom I've made a mistake, it's astounding to me how forgiving most humans are. With all that we have discussed regarding putting the prospect in the driver's seat, and having the prospect feel good about taking the next step with us, note that when we drop the ball, forget to communicate or avoid communicating potentially bad news, we only see things from our own perspective. We get locked up emotionally. We become proud or indignant and try to talk our way out of it with everyone, except the person with whom we should actually have the conversation.

The times I or people I have worked with have admitted errors, took the risk of having to share potentially bad news with a prospect or customer, the end result has always been the same: People will tend to forgive you.

They may not be happy about the issue, but they are much more appreciative of finding things out in advance or getting an explanation, than having to live in the dark and figure things out on their own.

Admitting to my kids that maybe I made a mistake by overreacting to an issue, or admitting to my wife that I was wrong about something only tells them that I have more in common with them. It reinforces the fact that I'm not perfect, no matter how much I aspire to do great things. It draws them closer to me. It shows them that a relationship is not a constant New Year's Eve party. It will have high points and low points, but it requires both people's involvement and both people's consideration of the other in order to survive.

Same goes for the relationships you make in selling. If you admit to there being high and lows, and that you might have to admit to mistakes once in a while, you'll find that both prospects and clients will respond better to you. And you'll be able to move more conversations forward.

Parenting and Other Impossible Jobs

When my two children were younger (my daughter was 6, my son was 8) it occurred to me that I was successful in dealing with adults but needed to start making a deep, lasting connection with my children. Kids have forgiving hearts and relentless optimism. In addition to their curiosity, they're not hindered by or burdened with distractions from genuine emotion. When they feel something, they let you know. If they want to know something, they ask and if they make an observation, they share it. Neither polite society nor parental embarrassment have the ability to stifle their curious honesty.

I realized that my son asked me many questions while I asked him very few. I'd been a father for eight years and had never thought to ask my kids questions. I started asking them questions while driving in the car. This didn't go over so well, so I tried asking during a meal.

"Dad, I don't wanna talk. I wanna eat now," my son informed me. It took time and great effort on my part to find a way to get my kids to talk to me. Eventually, I found that the time right after they went to bed, but before they fell asleep, provided the perfect opportunity. I'd lie on the floor and let them start talking to me about their day.

In the dark, we had no eye contact and no ability to read each other's body language. My son would tell me amazing things. Sometimes he'd ramble and there wouldn't be any dramatic revelations. Other times he'd tell me about what another kid did or said to him at school. Other times he'd tell me what he was thinking about at dinner when his mother and I were talking. I started the same thing with my daughter not too long after this and, even though she was younger, she enjoyed it.

The combination of them being in their own beds, in their own rooms, and the anonymity of the darkness (coupled with me offering no criticisms or advice) gave them a sense of freedom to express themselves that I believe was almost as valuable to them as it was to me.

Our relationship as father and son (and father and daughter) was truly redefined. They told me things during these talks that I wouldn't have discovered in other settings. I was no longer the authority figure at the head of the dinner table or the person insisting that they sit in a car seat or that they buckle their seat belt.

Because I listened to them intently, regularly, and did not interrupt, they saw me as a different person and I saw them as people with lives, thoughts and opinions as opposed to seeing them only as little kids.

We did not do this every night. We established a code for wanting to participate, and I'd go in and lie on the floor while they talked. One of us would say: "Can we talk tonight?"

As my children became older, the things we'd grown comfortable talking to each other about had a huge impact on our individual relationships. I now view being a parent as being part of a relationship with my kids, individually. It was not a "Do this, Don't do that" conversation I would conduct with these young people.

I learned the power that patient, silent listening afforded me, and now I felt compelled to apply it to other key, potentially rewarding relationships in my life. I'm not the perfect parent; I am, however, someone who has made a deep, long-lasting and personal connection with two other people who live in my house.

I look at my kids and see well-adjusted, smart, moral humans with a good sense of humor. I see, in their future, an ability to connect with people easily. Ultimately, I see people who will be respected, and eventually, adults to admire.

> I've learned more about being an adult by raising children than I think I could learn doing anything else. I've also learned more about selling by being a husband and father, than I have working a sales desk or closing deals with employees or trainees.

Relationships with customers, peers and kids all require consistency—not consistency of mood but consistency of intent and expectation. If you expect yourself to be professional and you say or do something that is inappropriate, you lose ground.

Major clients have been lost because the salesperson views certain things as appropriate and the client does not agree. It's not our clients' responsibility to give us a list of things they like, don't like or that they approve of or disapprove of.

Relationships are troubling, quirky, unpredictable and surprising things. They are created, maintained and ended by specific actions. They are initiated out of wonder, and set off course out of misunderstanding or inconsistency. They are fraught with (and sometimes defined by) emotions. Emotions, by definition, are not logical, and we get into trouble when trying to deal with an emotional situation using only logic.

 Remember: To maintain a relationship, treat it as though it has basic needs for survival and its survival is more dependent upon you than the other person. These basic needs are care, attention, as well as a sense of what is appropriate and what is not.

You don't have a crystal ball to consult in order to learn what other people think or feel. You do, however, have a great and reliable tool—communication—which is the third essential life skill. If both parties are interested and committed to the relationship, it has a greater chance for survival. Maintaining a relationship is one of the things that make us feel alive.

People need to be connected. At work, at home…in the world at large. One of life's great mysteries is how we are built for relationships and yet we must work so hard to maintain and enjoy them.

Some argue that the key to maintaining relationships is being able to overlook the faults and shortcomings of other people.

As a salesperson, if you look someone in the eye and tell him that you don't know everything, but are willing to try to find out any answer he might need, then his perception of you changes from someone trying to wrestle something away from him to someone who's looking to offer him something that will be of value.

To review some key concepts we've covered:

- Managing expectations means making sure you remain in step with what the other person wants to do next;

- Knowing when to back off can be the greatest application of sensitivity and compassion; and

- Seeing the other person as having things in common with you means acknowledging that people aren't perfect, don't know everything and will rarely do or say something to intentionally hurt you.

All of these are integral to the sales conversation because throughout that conversation, you are simultaneously:

➡ Thinking about how well (or poorly) the conversation is going.

➡ Thinking about where the conversation is going.

➡ Thinking about the next thing to say or ask.

➡ Thinking about how not to think about the potential commission that might come as a result, if the conversation progresses.

So, relationship management requires attention, intent, invention and submission. Submitting to what someone else wants does not translate into being subservient. You can submit to your spouse without feeling as though you've lost their respect or any authority. You can submit to a client without feeling as though the client is in charge of your life.

And you can be inventive, setting a new stage for each relationship, by asking prospects and customers what they would like to see happen next.

> People need relationships no matter how difficult they may be to maintain. You must hear people out and ask questions about them. One of the most difficult, yet rewarding things we can do as humans is give someone else our total and complete attention for any period of time.

Essential Life Skill 3: Communicating Clearly

When selling, you are free to do business with whomever you choose. The same is true with friends, lovers and acquaintances. You may be assigned a customer base but you will tend to do well with people with whom you connect.

Very early in life, we are culturally taught several things. We are taught the culture of our home and the correct way to react and respond to other people. The family culture takes us on regular, unpredictable emotional tours. We are closer to the people we live with than anyone else, for a good portion of our lives.

> The emotional tours we go on with the people we live with begin very early in life and those experiences impact and shape the way we communicate with the outside world.

Our parents or primary caregivers during our formative years are charged with teaching us several life-sustaining tasks: how to walk; how to feed ourselves; and how to talk. Although we're taught the mechanics of communication (i.e., how to form sentences), we are not taught *how* to communicate. We're taught how to let the outside world know that we want certain things but we are not taught the skills we are discussing in this book.

The world is not interested in your getting everything you want. It's not interested in supplying satisfaction to your every need. That's the job of a four-star resort.

Nor does the world feel obligated to provide you with protection. We are expected (and left) to fend for ourselves when it comes to basic sustenance, housing and so on.

But without connection to and with other people, our lives become dull, painful and empty. We must connect with others; we must communicate! Communication is a skill that can be learned. Since it can be learned, it follows logically that there must be a point of reference we can look to for guidance. For a measuring stick, we need some facts, figures and reassurances.

The 80/20 Principle

Recall what the 80/20 principle (according to Pareto) tell us:

- Eighty percent of any economy's gross product comes from 20 percent of the contributing industries.

- Eighty percent of the revenue generated by a company, is generated by 20 percent of the company's operating divisions.

We also have learned that 80 percent of a salesperson's income comes from 20 percent of that salesperson's activity. Our application of the 80/20 principle to communication skills, states:

Move the Sale Forward

- Eighty percent of your job as a salesperson (and skilled communicator) is to listen.

- Twenty percent of your job as a salesperson is *not* to talk, sell, overcome objections or close.

- Twenty percent of your job is to *respond*.

Keep in mind that responding and reacting are not the same. If you react to what someone says, then that puts you in a defensive mode. But, if you *respond* to what someone says, then you don't have to *prepare* or rehearse an answer. You don't have to look for an opportunity to hurry up and sell. When you are listening well enough to *respond* instead of *react*, whatever comes out of your mouth is perceived as more relevant to the conversation—especially if the response is based on the core of what *someone else's* message is.

☞ **Point of Impact #9:** Sales people are more interested in what they plan to say next than what is being said to them. Rephrased in the positive: Be more interested in what is being said *to* you than in planning what you're going to say next.

This is why so many sales conversations—and, ultimately, relationships—falter. When we're too busy preparing what we're going to say next, we forget to listen and make those human connections.

Since 80 percent of our job involves listening, curiosity about and genuine interest in people are key to being successful in selling (and in many other endeavors like parenting, friendships and relationships overall).

The Core of Your Message

The process of selling is based on the art of conversation and the skill of communicating. We've established the 80/20 principle as the cornerstone of effective communication. In order for you to have a positive, progressive exchange of ideas with people, it's your responsibility to understand and keep track of the core of your message. How do you make sure you and your prospect or customer are talking about the same thing? How do you ensure that you are responding to what is most important to your prospect or customer?

Answer: Listen to the last eight words that they say for the emotional impact of their message. Whether someone likes to paint word pictures or use analogies, whether they use stories to make their point or are a person of few words, one thing is true:

When someone wants to make a point, she tends to build up to it with data. So, the last eight words mean the most. (It *may* be factual, it *may not* be, but in the speaker's mind, progress is being made because she has the floor). Regardless of the validity of her info, if she believes it, that's all you have to work with.

Too many sales people feel the need to "educate the market" by selling a particular thing.

The market, however, is not waiting for you to educate it. Decision makers want to be knowledgeable and they (for the most part) want to make good, informed decisions, but when you go out armed with all of your pertinent and unequivocally correct data, the last thing a buyer wants is to listen to a prepared dissertation. Especially if it challenges what they are convinced of. Or worse, if the dissertation is delivered before the salesperson has learned anything about the customer.

> Educating is not feeding information or convincing or changing perception. In its most useful application, educate means to draw out—to have an exchange of

> information that moves from one person to the other through listening and responding.

Don't forget about Point of Impact #5: The more you listen to what someone has to say, the more fascinating he or she will find you. In effect, this entire book is about communicating. Our extensive discussion earlier regarding the power of silence and the 80/20 principle are profoundly important in the sales conversation. This principle, however, has applications in many other communications as well. Our definition of *communication*—the positive, progressive, exchange of ideas—is one that my children challenge me on regularly.

Communication is listening and responding. It's finding a way to put the other person's concerns before our own. It's intrinsic to the maintenance of any relationship. It's essential if we're going to master the skills of maintaining relationships and the skill of finding work.

Conclusion

Each of the three life skills—finding work, maintaining relationships and communicating—is dependent upon the other, to provide you with the tools you'll need to successfully navigate interaction with others.

When you work on developing your communication skills, you have a better chance at maintaining relationships. It follows, then, that when you communicate better and maintain relationships, it won't be as intimidating an enterprise to find work. Your friends may not be in the position to help you find work, but they can provide support.

Why do we talk about finding work at such length here? Why are we walking through these points regarding maintaining relationships and communicating? Because these are not only the essential skills to succeed in life—they are the essential skills required to succeed in sales.

Sales people must apply these skills every day.

Cold calling is, in effect, looking for work. Whether the salesperson is selling a product, a service or themselves as a vendor, they're always looking for work. Since it's a realistic expectation that some customers or assignments may not last forever and that their departure is rarely done with a lot of notice, sales people live under the specter of a portion of their income going away at any given time.

Finding work is not only applicable to interviewing for a position or mailing out résumés. It's the ongoing responsibility of the professional salesperson. Maintaining relationships is not "in addition" to the basic job description for sales people—it's a required asset.

Communicating, not pitching, is the core of the profession, from beginning to end—from soup to nuts.

Move the Sale Forward

CONCLUSION

So, where do you think you should go from here? By now, your first gut response should be: *Forward.*

As I write this, September 11, 2001 is over a year past and the American economy still stings from the decline of public trust in corporate giants. At the same time, however, people are closing deals, building businesses, establishing and maintaining relationships…and moving sales forward.

You now have an opportunity to join these folks in redefining the state of the economy, the perception of the profession, and most importantly, *your income potential* by applying what we've discussed. You can, and must demonstrate your ability to protect and provide for yourself and your family. My goal in these pages has been to remove the mystery from the selling process—not to attempt to make it appear easy. Removing the mystery from the process and taking the anxiety away regarding where your next deal will come from changes the way you approach each day.

These are challenging times. These times call for bold steps.

I encourage you to take confident, productive steps forward.

The world is looking—waiting—for some new great ideas. The fact that the U.S. patent office almost closed in the late 1800's because people believed there was "nothing left to invent" shows how we as humans can be both shortsighted and pompously arrogant about what we have, what we have to offer and what we may achieve. Avoid negativity. Embrace challenge. Do something no one else has done. Sounds easy, right?

Keep these goals in mind:

- *Move the sale forward.* This is the goal to always keep in mind.

- *Ask an open-ended killer question.* Be thoughtful, passionate and grab people's attention.

- *Make the human connection.* Bring what you have discovered in these pages to every conversation you have once you put this book down. If you make human connections, you will set yourself and your business apart.

Of the many books I have enjoyed over the years, the ones that touch me stay with me. I re-read them. I recommend them. I talk about what I got out of them with others who've read the same book. I only hope that this book becomes a topic of conversation among sales people. And I want our relationship to go on beyond the turning of the last page.

Now that you have come this far with me, let's continue the journey. I am always on the lookout for how people apply what I teach. Have a new insight or a success story about the 20 Call Burst? Let me know. Developed a great opening that sets a huge account in motion? Make some noise about it! Developed a list of open-ended killer questions that put mine to shame? Get them over to me.

You and I have got to help, encourage, discipline, instruct, motivate, humor and ultimately support each other.

Send me an e-mail with comments, ideas, results, horror stories or anything else you like! Here's my address: john@klymshyn.com.

When my editor asked me to write a conclusion to the barrage of ideas, techniques, examples and steps discussed in this book, I had a hard time accepting the notion of a conclusion. "Conclusion" sounds danger-ously like the end of something. My hope is that your experience with this book is the beginning of something.

Only you can determine what that is.

One More Exercise

Imagine a leather briefcase sitting on the floor at your side. Imagine 12 small, square boxes scattered next to it.

Each of the boxes is labeled with an attribute of yours. These at-tributes are:

- ☐ Experience
- ☐ Knowledge
- ☐ Energy
- ☐ Curiosity
- ☐ Humility
- ☐ Decisiveness
- ☐ Passion
- ☐ Dreams
- ☐ Vision
- ☐ Memory
- ☐ Strength
- ☐ Humor

Which of these is most valuable to you? Take that box and put it in your bag. Then, do the same with the one you deem the second-most valuable. Repeat this with the next most important on the list. Continue this mental process until all 12 boxes have been placed safely in the bag.

Looking into the bag, you see that the boxes have opened, and each attribute has escaped its box and is mixing with each of the others to form something new, exciting and *powerful*. Now realize that what sets you apart as a human is the ability to bring each of these attributes back out of the bag at will and apply them to whatever situation you face.

Now imagine that you bring this bag to your next appointment, whether that appointment is with the other parents of your kids' athletic team, or to a sales appointment or on your next interview while you search for work.

Which of these attributes is going to be of most interest or use to the people you see on these appointments?

You don't get to look in the bag and decide. There is only one way to find out what other people think, want, hope for, value, feel passionate about or believe.

If I have done my job with this book, you already know how to find that out, but I will reiterate:

Ask them. Ask *them*.

If you got nothing else out of this book, I hope you got a breather. I hope you took the time to stop and re-think your old selling tactics because now you are well-equipped with a new set of professional selling skills that will transform your career…and your future.

Good luck!

John Klymshyn
The Business Generator
December, 2002
Santa Clarita, California

APPENDIX A:

THE NINE POINTS OF IMPACT

☞ **Point of Impact #1:** When a potential customer hears an idea come out of your mouth, he hears an opinion. When he hears it come out of his own mouth, he hears facts or great ideas.

☞ **Point of Impact #2:** The first person to ask three questions in a row has taken control of the conversation.

☞ **Point of Impact #3:** The best way to direct a conversation is to keep some kinds of emotion out of it, while using others to forward the conversation.

Move the Sale Forward

☞ **Point of Impact #4**: The appropriate time to celebrate the sale is after the commission check clears your bank.

☞ **Point of Impact #5**: The more you listen to what others have to say, the more fascinating they'll find you.

☞ **Point of Impact #6**: The third time you begin a sentence with the word "I" is when your listener loses interest.

☞ **Point of Impact #7**: The salesperson who knows when to go away lives to sell another day.

☞ **Point of Impact #8**: If you have nothing and you risk that nothing and lose that nothing, you've lost nothing. But if you don't risk anything, you won't win anything, either.

☞ **Point of Impact #9**: Sales people are more interested in what they plan to say next than what is being said to them. Rephrased in the positive: Be more interested in what is being said to you than in planning what you're going to say next.

Move the Sale Forward

Appendix B:
Your Killer Questions

The components—building blocks—to killer questions include open-ended words (following a *Do* word with a *Don't* word); qualifiers; emotional trigger words; and action verbs. Keep these building blocks in mind when formulating your questions.

Open-ended (Do's)	Closed (Don'ts)
Who	Is
What	Can
When	Will
Where	Do
Why	Does
How	Could, Would, Should
Which	Has, Have
	If
	Are

Sample Qualifiers

Important	Productive	Efficient	Reasonable
Valuable	Often	Effective	Critical
Useful	Beneficial	Crucial Impact	

Sample Emotional Trigger Words

like	want	feel	think
believe	understand	agree	enjoy
hope	love	help	desire

Sample Action Verbs

solve	avoid	do	evaluate	choose
fix	accomplish	measure	investigate	learn

Use the worksheet on the following pages to write out your killer questions. You can tear this out of the book and keep it close to you throughout your selling day.

Your Killer Questions

1)_____?

2)_____?

3)_____?

4)_____?

5)_____?

6)_____?

7)_____?

8)_____?

9)_____?

10)_____?

11)_____?

12)_____?

13)_____?

14)_____?

15)_____?

Move the Sale Forward

16)_____?

17)_____?

18)_____?

19)_____?

20)_____?

21)_____?

22)_____?

23)_____?

24)_____?

25)_____?

APPENDIX C:

YOUR 20 CALL BURST

Use the following worksheet to fill in the names and numbers of the prospects and contacts you'll call on your next round of a 20 Call Burst. And get calling…today!

Name	Number
1)_____	_____
2)_____	_____
3)_____	_____
4)_____	_____
5)_____	_____
6)_____	_____
7)_____	_____
8)_____	_____
9)_____	_____

Move the Sale Forward

10)_____   _____

11)_____   _____

12)_____   _____

13)_____   _____

14)_____   _____

15)_____   _____

16)_____   _____

17)_____   _____

18)_____   _____

19)_____   _____

20)_____   _____

1)_____   _____

2)_____   _____

3)_____   _____

4)_____   _____

5)_____   _____

6)_____   _____

7)_____   _____

8)_____   _____

9)_____   _____

10)_____   _____

11)_____   _____

12)_____   _____

13)_____   _____

14)_____   _____

15)_____   _____

16)_____   _____

Move the Sale Forward

17)_____   _____

18)_____   _____

19)_____   _____

20)_____   _____

Notes:

_____
_____
_____
_____
_____
_____
_____
_____
_____
_____
_____
_____
_____
_____
_____
_____
_____
_____
_____
_____

Appendix D:

The Phone and Your Successful Job Search

The most effective tool for your successful job search is probably one that you haven't used to its fullest potential yet. More and more business leaders are making decisions and communicating with people over the phone. If you are out of work, or just looking, here are some tips on how you can create a more focused, successful job search by using the world's most powerful business machine—and it's right there in your home.

❶ **Prepare**: If you want to use the phone to make contacts, find out about openings, introduce yourself or follow up on an interview, the first thing you want to do is prepare beforehand. Know who you are going to call on a given day, and what you want as a result of each call. You have to plan ahead.

❷ **Change the focus**: What makes looking for a job difficult is that we tend to make ourselves the focus. We think about what we want, how much we want to earn, and most importantly, how uncomfortable we are in going out and asking for a job. No one likes having to ask for anything—we feel less confident and that affects how well we interview. By changing our focus, I mean that we should focus on what we do, how valuable it is and how much of a benefit that service would be to a given employer.

Move the Sale Forward

❸ **Be disciplined**. When you sit down to start calling, have already prepared 20 names to call (see previous worksheet). Think about it. Whatever you do, there must be at least 100 companies in reasonable commuting distance that could benefit by having you work there. Do your research, as I mentioned in step 1, and have those 100 names. Call 20 companies each day until you have contacted everyone. The interviews will come. The offers will come and within a short period (probably about four to six weeks) you'll be working at a new position.

❹ **Stay for the long haul**. Four to six weeks may sound like a long time, but you must allow for the time it will take to make an appointment for a first interview, to actually do the interview, be called back to meet others and to get an offer. We must keep generating activity and keep going on interviews until we have a bona fide offer and a day to start work. Anything, no matter how great it sounds, can fall through. Don't stop going on interviews because you came across something you really want and it's taking them some time to make up their minds.

❺ **Work on your communication skills**. Attend a sales seminar, even if you are not in sales, because an interview process is one where you sell yourself to several people. Failing attending a seminar, the library has plenty of books that you can read for free on the subject of sales.

❻ **Stay away from naysayers**. If you are part of a group that is made up of unemployed people and no one is getting anywhere, there is probably a reason for that. Get around people that are making something happen. Don't sit around feeling sorry for yourself and sharing bad news with others. Most people, when you tell them you are going to try something new, will give you several reasons why it won't work. *Don't listen to them*, because they are talking more to themselves than to you.

So, there you have it. Six things you can start implementing today to have a positive impact on your work search.

Sharpen your pencil, limber up that dialing finger…and get to work!

> **Use the telephone for work search success. It's among the most effective and available tools for you to use.**

Move the Sale Forward

Index